# JUSTICE FOR CODY

By Natalie Agnew

First published in 2015 by
The Solopreneur Publishing Company Ltd
Cedars Business Centre, Barnsley Road, Hemsworth, West Yorkshire WF9 4PU
www.thesolopreneur.co.uk



ISBN 978-0-9927840-6-5
Printed in the U.K.

Dedicated to Cody

## ACKNOWLEDGEMENTS

A big thank you to the following who helped with the book to...

Gail Powell, publisher, for approaching and presenting me with the opportunity to share and publish Cody's story.

Justin and Jake, my sons, who for being of such a tender age allowed their heartfelt emotions to be expressed in the book.

Paul O'Grady; for the passionate Foreword.

Simone Knocker and her son Matthew, for being such wonderful friends and for all their support and help with the administration.

Steven Agnew, the Green Party MLA; for his political input.

Mary Crooks, my mum, for all her help and support with the book.

# Contents

**FOREWORD by Paul O'Grady**

**About:**

Paul O'Grady

**About the author:**

Natalie Agnew

**INTRODUCTION:**

Why This Story Needs To Be Told by Gail Powell

**CHAPTER ONE:**

The Victim's Report

Police Case File

**CHAPTER TWO:**

Cody, The Puppy

**CHAPTER THREE:**

The Day It Happened

**CHAPTER FOUR:**

The Aftermath On Facebook

Messages By Letter and Cards

**CHAPTER FIVE:**

The Trial

What The Newspapers Reported

**CHAPTER SIX:**

What The Judge Had To Say

**CHAPTER SEVEN:**

A Political Perspective To Animal Cruelty

by Steven Agnew – The NI Green Party

**CHAPTER EIGHT:**

What's Next?

## Foreword by Paul O'Grady

On my TV show, 'Paul O'Grady's Animal Orphans', I visited Africa, looking at the plight of rhinos being hunted and killed for some perceived value in their horns. Animals that once roamed freely rarely survive nowadays outside of reserves and national parks.

Somebody once said that it's our duty on this planet to treat all animals with love and compassion. I don't know who that was, but obviously they haven't seen what goes on.

You may be reading this in the comfort of your home far from that country and thinking, "Well, that's Africa for you." Too far away for you to particularly worry about this type of behaviour, although I'm sure every animal-loving human being would feel sad for their plight. There may even be a pang of disappointment as to what humans can be capable of when it comes to the animal kingdom we have a duty to protect.

Cruelty to animals doesn't just happen

far, far away – it occurs in practically every country in the world, including yours. Many people who know me will be aware of how much I love and adore dogs – you may have seen my TV show 'For the Love of Dogs'. When I heard about what happened to the adorable collie dog, Cody, it sadly reminded me that animal cruelty happens much closer to home. In this particular instance, Northern Ireland - and to family pets we love and adore. Cody's only crime was to try to befriend every human she met, hoping to give love and receive it in return.

A treasured family pet that followed the wrong people, on the wrong day, simply for some love and attention - rewarded with an act of complete and utter mindless cruelty. Two young men, whose thought patterns for their actions most of us cannot even contemplate, not only ended Cody's life that day, but also devastated a family. It left two boys, who loved their beautiful pet dog, scarred for life.

Where does the law stand on this? Not as strong as it should be, that's for sure. So I salute anyone who is willing to go out there and campaign for harsher sentences that could act as a stronger deterrent.

I'm not sure where Natalie Agnew found the will to go on, what she must have gone through and is still experiencing, but this story needs to be told so that it doesn't happen again. I can only applaud her for her love and passion for animals, and for her endless campaigning to let the world know that this type of behaviour is just not acceptable. I wish Natalie all the luck possible with her endeavour to get 'Cody's Law' established. Anything that will further ensure that the punishment truly fits the crime, but better still, to hopefully make future perpetrators of animal cruelty think twice before they act, has to be a good thing.

**Paul O'Grady**

## About Paul O'Grady

Since 3 September 2012, Paul O'Grady has presented the ITV documentary series For the Love of Dogs, covering life at Battersea Dogs and Cats Home. Paul commented that he had wanted to do such a show for years and that he took to it with an "enthusiasm that surprised everyone, except me". At the end of the first series, Paul was invited to become an ambassador for Battersea Dogs and Cats Home in 2013. A bronze statue of his late dog, Buster, was erected on a plinth at the centre. He also adopted a dog from the home, a Jack Russell-Chihuahua cross named Eddy.

Paul has supported many philanthropic causes and joined the Pedigree Feeding Brighter Futures campaign, which aims to give a million meals to rescue dogs nationwide.

A donation amount from the sale of each

book will go to Battersea Dogs and Cats Home and a number of other canine charities supported by Natalie Agnew.

For more information about Paul O'Grady go to Wikipedia.org.

## About the Author – Natalie Agnew

Natalie Agnew lives at home in Northern Ireland with her two children, Justin and Jake, and their two border collies, C.J. and Rex. Natalie has always been an animal lover and lists her hobbies like horse-riding and walking her dogs. Her passions involve all matters concerning conservation, and more recently, her campaigning to bring about 'Cody's Law': a national campaign to increase sentences for perpetrators of animal cruelty.

This is Natalie's first book and is based on true life events.

Follow Natalie on Facebook:
www.facebook.com/justiceforcodythedog

## INTRODUCTION

***By Gail Powell - Publisher***

Some stories need to be told. Some stories are difficult to read. If we choose to ignore the inhuman actions that invade our world by human beings who have little regard for the animals we share this planet with, what does that say about us?

That said, however, I must confess that this was a story that both shocked and upset me to my very core, and I found very difficult to read. A dog owner, of border collies no less, my husband started following Cody's page from the day Natalie put up the first post about this abhorrent act of human cruelty against a defenceless pet dog.

I wholly admit that I struggled to listen to the details of what had happened that awful morning and the two weeks while Cody fought for her life. I do truly understand those people who have posted on the Justice for Cody Facebook page how much they want to support Natalie and the book, but how they would find it just too difficult to read. I ask you to trust in the process that we have gone through to make this happen and hopefully the following may encourage you even more to read on.

My husband was relentless in his desire that I published Natalie's story, perhaps one of the hazards of owning a book-publishing business, although I knew he was right! There were two reactions: Firstly, could I do this, as I would have to read everything and see the pictures? This was something I'd largely managed to avoid; secondly, I felt burdened with a great responsibility to ensure that this was the best book it could be under the circumstances. I was concerned that it would do the job it was supposed to do - to help people make some sense of what happened and not sensationalise the story in any way. As the publisher, I also had to ensure the book was not only honest but sensitive, and that it would encourage the reader to support Natalie with her Cody's Law campaign. It was paramount that the message was heard loud and clear that the law needed changing; to enforce stricter sentences for animal cruelty.

When I approached Natalie my main aim was to help her revisit the events in a truthful, but unsensational way, in the hope that it stops something like that ever happening again. I sincerely hope this book goes some way towards helping Natalie achieve her goal of getting Cody's Law passed. And perhaps, even in a small way, provide some closure for Natalie and her lovely family.

It had taken two years before I approached Natalie because it would have been impossible to write this book until the two perpetrators were brought to justice. This eventually happened towards the end of 2014, but what justice! At the time of printing, one of the perpetrators is already out of prison after serving only a few months.

It's funny, sometimes, how life can be. Because of this meaningless and cruel crime I've got to know Natalie and completely understand the impact this has had on her and her family. I feel blessed to have met Natalie and to help her in her quest.

This book is made up of Natalie's own words, the judge's reports, court and case notes, stories from the newspapers covering the story, and some of the Facebook posts and comments the family received. There's also a chapter from Steven Agnew (no relation), the leader of the Northern Ireland Green Party, who has supported Natalie for a long time. He is also on a quest: to create a register of animal cruelty offenders that will stop them from ever owning pets again, or from working with or around animals. You can find out more in chapter seven.

I was overwhelmed when I approached Paul O'Grady's management and asked if he would consider writing the foreword for the book. They came back immediately, having asked him, and his response was a resounding 'yes'. Paul has a fabulous media platform where he can be seen and heard more than many of us, and he's not afraid to put it to good use. His love of all animals, especially dogs, made him the perfect choice. So, a very big 'thank you', Paul, from the bottom of our hearts, and for all the work you continue to do to help the animal kingdom.

Suffice to say, some of what you're about to read will pull at your emotions but, hopefully, we have handled this with care. It's a responsibility we've not taken lightly. I think what has made this story all the more poignant is that Maghaberry is such a quiet, small friendly village. The attack on Cody, by two of its very own residents, shocked and horrified this small community. The locals of the village were appalled that there were two evil, cruel, and potentially dangerous men living on their very doorstep. Ultimately did they get the sentences they deserved – without exception the many supporters of Natalie and her family through all this would unite in their response to a resounding 'no!'

Thank you for reading this book and supporting Natalie, the Agnew family, and most of all, Cody – whose life was cut mindlessly short. We promise to make her life mean something and our promise to Cody ... 'we will never forget you'.
We hope one day very soon to publish a revised edition that announces the passing of Cody's Law.

# CHAPTER ONE: THE VICTIM'S REPORT

To Judge McFarland

I can't explain in words how horrendous it was to open my back door that morning of Cody's attack, and on her return to be hit by an intense smell of burning flesh, so strong and pungent. Cody was only a small resemblance to her former self, standing in front of me, staring up at me, nose burnt raw to the flesh. One eye blood-red, her body covered in raw, burnt fleshy patches and blood dripping from her body. Her hair was practically all singed off and she looked half her size. I knew instantly that someone had set fire to her. This memory will haunt me forever; it never fades and neither has the shock. I still feel it as strongly today. Cody feared no-one and trusted everyone. Unfortunately, this was to be to her detriment.

Cody's horrendous attack has consumed all our lives for two years. It's been a rollercoaster of emotions for all of us. The hardest part was having to break the awful news to our two young boys, then six and ten years old. They were upstairs when I found Cody; I had little time to think and I was in a state of shock. Cody was in excruciating pain and I knew she needed urgent medical attention. My husband, Martin, and I had no time to carefully choose our words, we had to just explain what had happened and did not have the luxury of softening the blow. They were both inconsolable and asked questions we were unable to answer, all the time we were trying to keep ourselves calm as well as calming them.

During the two-week period of Cody's fight for survival the vet had hope that she may survive; although she would have needed a back leg amputating, there was still a chance she would come through it. I decided to allow the boys to visit her at the vets every day. Justin was afraid to touch Cody for fear he would hurt her, and he found it difficult to even look at her with all her horrific burns. Jake constantly hugged her and talked to her; eventually, she refused food from everyone but accepted it from his hands, it was as if she didn't want to disappoint him. Jake's birthday was approaching and he asked for his only present to be that Cody came to his party. We discussed this with the vet who agreed that, if she were stable enough, we could have her home for a few hours for the party. Unfortunately, this was not to be as, the following week, we got the dreaded phone call from the vet explaining that Cody was deteriorating rapidly. Her organs were failing and her flesh decaying. Her pain levels had increased and it was unethical to keep her alive any longer, as she'd experience a prolonged and painful death. We will never forget that awful day and having to break the news to the boys – another traumatic blow.

After Cody's death, Jake rapidly began to change. He was inconsolable, crying daily; he lost all interest in school, his friends, activities, and the sports he'd previously loved. He developed a fear of anything and everything and suffered from severe anxiety. He developed a fear of heights, even though he'd been jumping off the top board of the swimming pool from the age of four in his diving club. Jake eventually left the diving club, as his fear escalated.

Most worrying of all was when he started to look in the mirror at himself and say how ugly he was, asking how anyone could possibly like him. I realised, months later, why he felt this way. He broke down and explained to me that it was his fault Cody was attacked because he saw her in the garden before the two men came down the lane. He was punishing himself for not bringing her in. He hated himself for this. This broke my heart. No words could change his mind, no matter what we said it made no difference.

His friend was also suffering, going home from school and crying, telling his mum how sad Jake was all the time; he was so worried about him. When his friend asked Jake what was wrong, he answered "I want Cody back". Jake was petrified to go to school. He would tell me in great detail about the visions he had of two men bursting through the back doors of the school to get him. It also became something he feared would really happen. Jake changed from a bubbly, happy, funny boy, to a very quiet, sad boy.

Jake became very anxious and worried

if Martin or I were going anywhere for a weekend away. I was going away for a hen weekend 9 months after Cody's death and I was very close to cancelling it due to Jake's sheer panic at the thought of me getting on a plane. He was petrified that something would happen to me such as the plane crashing. He clung onto me for days before begging me not to go. I remember the night before as I was to leave at 5am that morning. I was putting him to bed and he wouldn't let go of me and begged me not to go. This broke my heart hearing the fear and anxiety in his voice at 7 years of age. Jake was constantly panicking that he would lose his parents as well as Cody.

I remember Jake asking me how Cody was set alight; this was a few weeks after Cody's attack. I had to explain that flammable liquids were poured over her and then they set her alight. This was horrific and I could barely say those words myself without an awful gut-wrenching, sickening feeling of actually having to say these words out loud. Jakes reply was " mummy it had to be an accident they couldn't have done that maybe they just dropped a cigarette on her and she caught fire?" I had to say "no Jake, unfortunately, that's what we would like to believe, but that wasn't the case with Cody's attack". Once again this was a heart-wrenching conversation that upset and angered me, this innocent young mind was searching for reasons for it to have been an accident. It was just too painful to digest the truth.

At this point, about a year after Cody's death, we decided he needed help. We took him for counselling, which helped greatly. It changed the way he thought and, most importantly, helped him to realise that it was not his fault. Jake slowly returned to the boy we knew.

We now recognise the signs if Jake starts to slip away again, and still occasionally arrange counselling for him. He still struggles and panics when we go on holiday and have to leave our two dogs in kennels, he gets very anxious and worries about them. He goes to bed at night surrounded by dog teddies all called Cody. He has a framed portrait of her, a poem wrote for Jake about Cody, and a beaded star a supporter made for him, which represents Cody - the brightest star in the sky. Wherever he goes, all this has to go with him. Otherwise, he can't sleep. Without a doubt, Jake has suffered the most trauma and is a constant worry, as he does slip back into his anxious state at times; this happens particularly when Cody is talked about by others, or when the incident catches the attention of the media. Following one such event Jake told me his heart was sore. I asked why, and he said "because of Cody". I asked Jake if he wanted to write a few words for this report, but he felt unable to, as it would have only made him cry.

Justin, our older boy, is far less in touch with his emotions and harder to read. Justin became withdrawn and angry as he found it difficult to express his emotions. He was only 10 years old at the time. He suffered nightmares, always constantly hearing footsteps approaching his room up the stairs. He thought it was the two culprits coming to back to get him. He was afraid to go upstairs alone even during the day. Justin was also afraid to go to the village to play outside with his friends;

afraid he would bump into the two culprits as they were still living in the village and out on bail. He was terrified that they would attack him. For months after the attack, Justin would walk back and forth to the kitchen window where he had a clear view to see if anyone were walking down the lane approaching our house. This became a constant habit. Justin very rarely talked about his emotions but would quite often ask a lot of questions about how and why Andrew and Jamie could do such a thing to an innocent animal.

Personally, I found the attack on Cody to be very traumatic. I don't think I will ever come to terms with it. I can't bear to think of the agonising pain Cody was forced to endure from the attack and for the two week afterwards. Writing this is very hard for me, as I've had to delve deep into the true effect it has had on me for two years. I very quickly threw myself, and my emotions, into finding the culprits and seeking justice. I set up a Facebook page: 'Justice for Cody', and the overwhelming amount of support and encouragement helped restore my faith in humanity. I felt reassured we were not alone in this fight for justice. I put all my efforts into fundraising for various animal charities, including Guide Dogs for the Blind. It's some consolation that Cody did not die in vain, she can hopefully make a difference to other animals and be remembered for that.

My aim was justice for Cody and my family: a prison sentence for the perpetrators. I hoped that the maximum sentence of two years would be a deterrent to other animal abusers, a clear message that behaviour like this will not be tolerated, and that there will be consequences.

Throughout the past two years, I have experienced despair, grief and anger. I've sometimes found it difficult to keep up the 'Justice for Cody' page at times, due to it being unbearably emotional. Another big effect was fear, when I heard that a witness was threatened I became very afraid and paranoid, and I still am at times. I found it hard to stay in the house on my own, I was so afraid of retaliation. I was worried I'd bump into the two men or their families, wherever I went.

I feel my boys need to see justice served. I don't want them growing up with more anger, wondering why there were no consequences in life for such wrong and evil actions. Another reason I want justice is for my own peace of mind, that I've done all I can, to get justice and possibly help prevent the two men from reoffending, or even worse. I would feel responsible if I didn't fight 100% for justice, even more so if I heard, further down the line, that their next victim was a child. Maybe, after the sentencing, we will have some kind of closure, but I know we will never forget or come to terms with Cody's attack. I feel the effects on my family will be ongoing. Every day I spend with my two new dogs is a constant reminder of Cody. As they look at me with total trust, I can't understand how anyone could abuse an innocent animal.

In the initial stages of the investigation after the attack, a story of events began to unfold very quickly. In a combined effort, involving the police investigator and the locals of Maghaberry community, a series of events started to take shape. All the pieces of the jigsaw that made up our case started to join together. From the day after Cody's attack, we had various people contacting us, either by phone or personally calling at our house, handing us handwritten names of the men suspected of the abuse. The police investigator had already narrowed suspects to five men known to be at an all-night party in the village the night before the attack. Within a week, the two suspects, Jamie Downey and Andrew Stewart, were identified. This first week was a bit of a blur - so much information was passed to us by members of the community. The police investigator was very thorough and determined to piece together all the evidence and witness accounts and bring the culprits to justice. Trying to keep Jake and Justin from hearing everything was difficult. We tried to keep as much information as possible from them, as they were already struggling to cope with the horrendous attack on Cody, and the two-week aftermath as she struggled to cling on to life. It was a very difficult time for us, visiting Cody daily at the vets, watching her suffer – hoping, each passing day, that she would make it.

# The Police Case File

## *R v Downey & Stewart: Outline of Case (Summarised)*

On Sunday 26th August 2012, at approximately 12:20 hours, Natalie Agnew reported to police via the 999 system that youths had set fire to her dog.

Prompt enquiries conducted with the dog's owner revealed that the dog, Cody, a three-and-a-half-year-old collie, was let out of the house to run around the front of the dwelling, at around 7:30 hours on the morning of Sunday 26th August 2012. At approximately 09:00 hours Mrs Agnew's son informed her and her husband that he had seen two males walking down the laneway towards their home. He stated that he had viewed them through the dining room window and watched them go towards an old quarry that's located close to their home. Mrs Agnew then went outside and checked to see if the males were still about, but they had left. She then called for Cody but got no response, and a search of the immediate vicinity for the dog proved negative. Sometime between 10:30 and 10:45 hours, while Mrs Agnew was in the kitchen, she noticed what she described as an animal in her back garden running towards the back door. When Mrs Agnew opened the door, she immediately smelled burning and recognised the animal to be Cody. The dog's skin was exposed and raw, and it was bleeding from various parts of its body, with a lot of fur missing; her joints were even visible through her burnt flesh. Mrs Agnew immediately phoned a local vet and took the dog to the surgery.

Cody was given intensive treatment for the burns caused to her body and face. She was put on strong pain relief and remained heavily sedated throughout the duration of her veterinary care. The vet, Mr Ian Moore, was of the opinion that an accelerant had been used to cause the dog's injuries. He informed the family that an accelerant or other flammable liquid had been poured onto Cody's back, which then dripped down her legs prior to being ignited. He added that Cody's face was burnt because she had probably instinctively turned her head towards the flames. On Saturday 8th September 2012, approximately two weeks after the initial incident, Cody was sadly put to rest, due to the horrific injuries she sustained. Her injuries would not heal and she was constantly in pain. Therefore, the family were left with no choice but to request euthanasia be humanely administered to prevent any further suffering.

A police investigation was instigated, and with the assistance of the Agnew family and members of the general public, mostly residents of Maghaberry village, information about who may have been responsible began to surface; a number of leads were followed up. Police concentrated their enquiries towards the possibility that the males Mrs Agnew's son spotted were residents of the village, and that they were finishing off their alcohol from a party the night before.

A substantial amount of information started to filter through to the police and the Agnew family; those who provided details were spoken to and their accounts examined for evidential value. From the information obtained, a picture soon started to emerge about the movements of the two males, noted by a number of people on the morning in question.

At approximately 10:00 hours two males were observed walking up Trummery Lane, near the quarry entrance and towards the village; these males were accompanied by a collie dog. They were then seen to enter the quarry and were out of sight. A check of old portacabins formerly used as labourers' accommodation was conducted, and a small quantity of singed, dark-coloured animal hair was discovered inside. As no scorch marks were located, and there were no signs of any fire, it's believed that Cody was set alight outside the buildings, running inside in her panicked and distressed state.

Further information soon materialised that a party had indeed occurred in the village on the night before the incident. The householder, Fiona Kelly, was interviewed, and although she had a good recollection of who was actually present at her party, her memory didn't stretch to remembering what they were wearing, drinking, or exactly when each person left her home.

A party-goer, Robert Quail, stated that fellow revellers Andrew Stewart and Jamie Downey did not leave the party until 09:00 hours and that they had gone for a walk before going home.

On Tuesday 4th September 2012, as a direct result of the evidence acquired and the inconsistencies in the explanations offered by Andrew Stewart and Jamie Downey when interviewed, both males were arrested for the suspected offence of animal cruelty. Andrew Stewart was asked directly on a number of occasions if he had set Cody on fire, or knew anything about the incident, to which he stated he did not. From the outset of the initial interview with Jamie Downey, during which time he had a solicitor present, it was apparent that he was not going to say very much. This was borne by the fact that his responses were continually guided by his solicitor's advice. He too was asked directly if he had set Cody on fire or knew anything about the incident; he also stated he did not.

As there were a number of enquiries, ongoing Andrew Stewart and Jamie Downey were bailed to return to Lisburn PSNI Station at a later date.

During this protracted investigation, a number of unfortunate events ensured that any prosecution against the two suspects would be difficult to serve. When police attended the home of the Agnew family and attempted to retrace the steps of the males seen around the house they recovered two barbecue lighting fluid bottles; these were removed for forensic examination. It was believed from the beginning that a flammable liquid was used on Cody. However, the examination of these bottles proved negative. CCTV obtained from Maghaberry Primary School confirmed the direction the two males had come from, prior to entering the Agnew's land, and that one was taller than the other, but the images provided were of a convex appearance. An attempt to enhance them also proved negative.

It was noted that the premises next door to the primary school, Masseys, had CCTV installed and that this was positioned closer to the footpath. Therefore, it was hoped the images would clearly identify the two males. Unfortunately, it transpired that, unbeknown to Masseys' owners, the CCTV had been defective for a year and had failed to record the suspects or anything else for that matter.

Also, the VIPER identification procedure carried out at an early stage of the enquiry failed to pick out the suspects, and the statements from the witnesses who could actually identify the males didn't come to light until the latter stages of the investigation. An empty 'Buckfast' bottle that was seen lying at the entrance to a field on Trummery Lane was not mentioned until a few days after the event, and when police attempted to retrieve this item for fingerprinting it had gone. The content of a mobile phone seized from Jamie Downey also failed to bear any significant findings.

At present, no forensic evidence is available that conclusively links the suspects to the dog, and any evidence that does exist is of a circumstantial nature. Despite the two suspects claiming no involvement in the incident, it's clear to see that they have been caught out by a number of conspicuous points.

From trawling through the information contained in this file, and as previously stated, it is glaringly obvious that no forensic evidence exists that incontestably ties in the alleged suspects to the actual crime. But what does exist is the fact the two defendants were seen and identified by witnesses.

Note to PPS

The interest generated by this incident was so great that it overshadowed a high-profile serious assault that occurred in the Lisburn area at the time. I believe this particular case would fall within the classification of what would be deemed to be in the public interest to prosecute. I, as the investigating officer, believe wholeheartedly that the two defendants arrested and subsequently interviewed carried out this vicious and abhorrent act on Cody. This view is not borne from a mere hunch or inkling, but from a scepticism and mistrust created by the mendacious comments provided by the suspects themselves during the overall investigation.

The incident itself caused a major outcry of disgust and revulsion from the general public of Northern Ireland, and even further afield. The matter was reported all over the world; media sources as far as America and Australia ran the story of this atrocious incident. Initially, the Agnew family set up a public appeal using Facebook, on a page entitled 'Justice for Cody', in an attempt to obtain information as to who was responsible for this deliberate and sadistic attack on a defenceless dog. The site has gained even more followers since and is now used to raise public awareness of animal cruelty incidents, and to raise money for animal-related charities.

The profound effect this incident has had is far-reaching, and the legacy it has left can be seen in the heartfelt message young Jake Agnew suddenly wrote nearly eight months after Cody was harmed. His penned note attempted to describe his feelings for his former pet and what was done to her. The message conveys the fear and worry he now holds for himself and his loved ones as a result of what happened. In a recent conversation with Natalie Agnew, she informed police that the family have had to seek the assistance of a counsellor to resolve Jake's anxiety.

# CHAPTER TWO: Cody, the Puppy

I've been passionate about all animals from a very young age and had rabbits, cats and a dog during my childhood. In my teenage years I strongly opposed animal cruelty; all my English debates were about animal abuse and I had many scrapbooks filled with horrific animal cruelty articles. This included reports on circus animals, seal clubbing, whale hunting, fox hunting, to name just a few. I'm strongly against animal testing for cosmetics and also abhor the fur trade – I even donated a few pounds of my pocket money every week to WWF. I remember reading animal cruelty cases and feeling distraught at any animal cruelty case I came across. I never in a million years thought I would be faced with such a cruel and barbaric attack on my own family pet. It was always something I read or heard about that happened to other people. To be faced with this situation is something I never expected to experience, considering I spent so many years trying to help animals and spread awareness of all forms of animal cruelty.

My family got a pet collie when I was thirteen, called Sally. Through my teenage years, she was my best friend, many a time I curled up beside her in bed and told her all my worries. She always sensed my mood and acted accordingly: calm and affectionate when I was upset, or responding with a playful nature when I was in high spirits. Sally came everywhere with me, and when I moved out to set up my own home with my husband to be, I brought Sally with me. At 16 years old, due to a liver tumour, Sally had to be put to sleep. I was devastated, she had been a huge part of my life. Five years had passed before I considered a new puppy. I felt no other could replace Sally but my family, with my two boys, Justin, then seven, and Jake, four, did not feel complete without a family dog.

We decided as a family that it was time for a puppy. Justin and Jake were very excited at the thought and we began to look out for collie pups. Martin and I both agreed; after having Sally, we wanted another collie because we feel they're intelligent and very loyal. We saw an advert in the local newspaper from a farming family looking for homes for a litter of collie pups near Tyrella Beach, Newcastle. We went to see the pups, and the last to be chosen was absolutely beautiful, and the only one with blue eyes. We instantly fell in love with her, she was so fluffy and affectionate. One week later we agreed we'd take her. After collecting her, we had to stop several times on the journey home - she vomited and had diarrhoea the whole way home. If we weren't stopping for her, it was because Jake had to vomit at the side of the road. I'd not thought about his gagging reflex at repulsive smells! So Jake and Cody's first trip in the car was not much fun.

Cody instantly became part of the family, although she was very difficult to toilet train. I found out six months later that she had campolobacter, which caused constant diarrhoea and bleeding; it was only after I was diagnosed with this did we realise it was what Cody had. Campolabactor is usually passed through sheep or food poisoning, but once infected, is highly contagious and can be fatal for the young and very old. I struggled with abdominal symptoms for six months afterwards; thankfully, the boys didn't become infected but Cody took a long time for her symptoms to settle. When they did, however, her training was much easier. Cody had a very infectious personality - everyone loved her, she was so excitable and loved any attention, and she feared no-one. Cody was loved by adults and children throughout the village; at the school runs and any opportunity in her first three years, she would escape and run to the village if the boys were in school. She would appear at the school front or back door wanting in, or if the kids were out in the playground she would be in the middle of the kids thinking it was great. She was obviously looking for Jake and Justin, though she occasionally ran to our neighbours where she was given red meat as a treat. They joked about this, as I only gave her chicken, not read meat. Cody also visited another family that had got a collie pup at the same time; she could be found wrestling in the garden with him. Jake loved Cody's goodnight cuddles. He'd lie beside her and wrap his arms around her and beg us to let her stay all night on his bed. We had to explain that Cody was so hyper, she'd keep him awake all night.

Justin loved playing football with Cody; despite all the balls she burst he still enjoyed kicking a ball around with her and playing fetch. Cody was much calmer around Justin, as he preferred to gently stroke her, whereas Jake liked to wrestle and cuddle up to her. Cody responded differently to the two boys' personalities.

We went for a week to Cushendall, up the Antrim coast. Our friends and their two boys, of similar age to Justin and Jake, came over and we hired a lovely house within walking distance of the beach. A farming family owned the property and the farmed land around us. Cody came with us, and the farmer took Cody with him to help round up sheep. Although Cody had never been a working collie, and even though she was only two years old, the farmer said she definitely had it in her to be a good working sheep dog. He'd had lots of experience with collies and trained many throughout his life. This came as a shock because we thought Cody was too excitable in nature for such a role. That week, the locals soon got to know Cody. Although we trusted her off the lead when walking on the beach, she'd decide to bolt out of the blue and make her way into a local café amid lots of people. This was like heaven to her! When we finally caught up with her, Cody already had an adoring fan club giving her lots of attention and food.

Cody was an integral part of our family and it felt like she'd always be there. We also had two cats, Rumple and Stiltskin, who we brought home from the Cats' Protection League a few months before we got Cody. All three were great friends, which is much easier to achieve when kittens are young. The cats ruled the roost, however!

Cody eventually stopped running away to the village at any opportunity, and we were able to let her have an hour or two unsupervised play. She had the run of the land around us while we were in the house; this was her routine in the mornings. We'd let her out for a while then bring her in again, she would always come to a window or door when she wanted to come back in. Cody had her routine and was truly settled by the time she was three-and-a-half. All that changed one

Sunday morning. Very quickly, her happy-go-lucky life was brought to an end.

# CHAPTER THREE: The Day It Happened

On Saturday 26th August, at around 11pm, we arrived home from a family holiday to Northumberland. At approximately 9am, the next morning Jake ran to our bedroom sounding very distressed and worried, explaining he saw two teenage boys walk down the private lane towards our house. They'd continued past the side of the house, as he watched from the playroom window. Jake then moved to the dining room to follow them on their path towards the back of the house. At this point, Jake explained that they'd looked around the property and towards the window he was standing behind. He'd instinctively ducked under the windowsill, out of sight.

Jake seemed very anxious and worried as he explained the details. He seemed to sense, even at six years old, that there was something scary about the two boys. He'd felt afraid when the boys looked towards him as he watched from the dining room and was the reason he crouched down under the window. Slowly, Jake emerged to see what they were doing and where they were going. He watched them continue to the back of the house and into the surrounding fields, towards a disused quarry that sits on our land.

After digesting Jake's words, I had an immediate sense that something was abnormal about the two teenagers walking down our lane and round the back of our house. I quickly got dressed and walked towards the quarry, calling Cody's name. We'd let her out at about 7:30 that morning, as per her daily routine, to run around the fields and our back garden for an hour or two every morning. I remember the awful thought that flashed through my mind - that someone had done something to Cody. I called and called her name, looking to see if I could find these two boys. I went up to the quarry and scanned my eyes across the fields. There was no sign of Cody or the two boys. At this stage, I thought perhaps the boys had been out walking and thought our lane was a public footpath, or that maybe they were lost. I knew that Cody, being so friendly and trusting, would have most probably followed them.

I went back to the house and began a few chores. I figured that if Cody didn't return home soon I would go the village and look for her. On my return, Jake became obsessed with these two boys. He seemed very anxious about them, constantly describing what the boys looked like; one was apparently very tall and the other was very small. He moulded his hair into the shape of both boys' hairstyles and described the colour of their hair, what they were wearing and their facial expressions. He would not stop talking about them. I told him to calm down and that everything was going to be okay. "But where's Cody?" he kept asking. I explained that Cody had possibly followed them but that she would be back soon.

Around 10:30am, Justin and Jake were upstairs in Justin's bedroom. Martin was pottering about downstairs, about to get into the car to go to the local shop, and I was standing at the kitchen window, doing dishes. The kitchen window overlooks the back garden and surrounding fields. What I saw running across the garden to our back door will stay with me until the day I die. At first I thought it was a wild animal escaped from the zoo, which was now in my back garden; this animal looked brown, skinny, and not normal. I opened the back door and a repulsive stench hit me - an intense burning smell; even though there was so much open space outside the smell was still strong. I quickly realised it was the smell of burning flesh. I barely recognised the animal to be Cody; her nose was burnt, she had big patches of red-raw flesh, and one eye was blood red. Most of her hair was gone, and what was left was singed, brown and covered in blood. Blood dripped from her body.

Cody stared at me in obvious agony. My hands flew to my mouth in horror then I started to scream. I knew instantly that someone had set her on fire. I ran from Cody upon hearing Martin's engine starting from the front of the house. I ran to catch him before he left. Cody scampered after me, obviously looking for help. I couldn't bear to look at her. The intense stench of burning flesh was everywhere.

Martin had just begun to drive off as I

ran behind him, flapping my arms in the air, in a desperate attempt to grasp his attention. Thankfully, he saw me through the rear view mirror and stopped the car. I screamed, "Someone has done this to Cody!" At this point, Cody ran to her kennel and lay down. Martin's face was just pure shock. He told me to grab a blanket to wrap her in; he'd get her into the car while I phoned the vet. I found a blanket and gave it to Martin - I couldn't go anywhere near Cody.

The pain and shock I felt was overwhelming. I realised I had to try and keep myself together. When I told the vet he was shocked himself, saying, "Someone did this, you think?" He said to go straight to the veterinary clinic and he'd join us in fifteen minutes; she'd need instant medical attention and all the equipment was there. When I came off the phone, Martin had managed to get Cody in the front of the car, on the floor, with a blanket.

We needed to tell the boys what had happened, and call Martin's parents, who live close by, to come and look after the boys while we went to the vets. We had no time to soften the blow, we were both in a state of shock ourselves. We said to the boys, “Someone has done something to Cody and hurt her really bad.” Jake burst out crying then Justin did the same, running to his bed to sob.

Jake asked, “Why?" We had no answers. We explained Cody was in the car and we needed to get her to the vets urgently. We had no time to console them, trying to keep ourselves calm was hard enough. The boys left with their nanny, and we ran to the car. I had to sit in the back - I couldn’t even look at Cody, it was too painful for me. The smell in the car was the same repulsive, strong stench; I kept my hands over my face and tried to cover my nose to block it out. I just couldn't bear the thought of how much pain Cody was in.

When we arrived at the vets, we parked right outside the door. Martin carried Cody as I lingered behind, still unable to look at her. Ian, the vet, was horrified when he saw Cody. He said he’d never come across such a barbaric attack. He could tell immediately that it had been done deliberately from the large patches where flammable liquid had been poured on her, and the drips down her legs. If it had been an accident, it would have appeared differently, with no patches.

I stayed in the waiting room while Martin took Cody into the treatment room. I was in total shock. Ian advised us to leave Cody with him. She'd lost a lot of blood and was dehydrated; she needed to go on a drip and be sedated for pain relief. We left Cody in Ian's care and decided to drive through the village, to see if we could see anyone hanging around suspiciously.

We stopped at Hammond Farm as I recognised Jo, a mother of one of Jake's friends from school, outside her house in her front garden. I wound down the window and the tears started falling instantly. I asked Jo if she'd seen anyone acting suspiciously. I explained what had happened; saying the words, "Someone has set fire to Cody" was overwhelmingly difficult. Jo was shocked but said she hadn't seen anything. We continued to drive around the village. I don't know what we were expecting or hoping to find, but we didn't see anyone or anything out of the ordinary. We then drove home.

We went up the side of the house to the quarry where, at this point, we believed the attack had taken place. We found a discarded lighter fluid tin lying on the ground and wondered if this was the flammable liquid used to set Cody alight. At this point, we phoned the police, but I remember thinking, "What's the point? What can they do?"

Despite our doubts, we reported the horrendous attack on Cody. The PSNI responded immediately and sent an investigating officer out to speak with us. The initial statement of events was recorded; the officer was genuinely horrified, and very sympathetic. We walked around the area, searching for any clues or evidence. The lighter fluid was taken as a potential source of evidence; this was all we found. The investigating officer explained that she would return the next day to follow up with enquiries; she left to report the incident back to the station.

After she'd gone, Martin and I discussed whether we believed anything would come from reporting Cody's attack, as we have little faith in the UK justice system. Martin was overcome with anger while I just sat in total shock. I began to ring around our family and close friends; they all loved Cody and I knew I had to let them know. Having to phone round everyone and explain what had happened over and over again was traumatising. They were all horrified and asked many questions I couldn't answer. Two friends, Simone and Diane, who often looked after Cody if we were away for the weekend, as devoted animal lovers, were beside themselves with grief. Diane only recently found my text to her which read:

*"Hi, Diane, someone set fire to Cody this morning in the quarry. She's in a really bad way; the police are coming out, I'm just so shocked. It's so awful, she's at the vets on a drip; he's going to keep her, we won't know how she's doing for a while. Just can't believe someone could do that."*

When I read this text sent over two years ago it sends chills down my spine. I remember phoning my brother, James, to explain what had happened at the time. He was in shock and just kept repeating, “You are joking. You’re joking, no way, no way."

I remember shouting, “I'm hardly joking,”, but I knew he was in shock and just couldn't take in the horrifying news. James had two dogs himself and I think, being a dog owner, and understanding the connection between a family pet and its owner, makes it even harder to comprehend.

The first week at the vets, Cody was much brighter than during the second week. Initially, her eyes were bright and she walked around the vets amongst all the other people coming in and out with their own pets. She received plenty of attention and everyone knew who she was and what had happened to her. The vet put a lot of effort into researching horrific burn treatments, as he’d never come across such horrific burn injuries before. Cody had to be covered in ointment and wrapped in clingfilm every day to help the burns heal and to prevent infection.

The problem was that we didn't know the depth of her burns until the dead, burnt skin came away. The first week, therefore, was a waiting game that we just had to take it day by day. The second week was not very hopeful; Cody was clearly deteriorating, she was unable to walk around anymore and refused food. The first sign for me that she was losing her fight for life was when she avoided contact with my eyes. She refused to look at me and kept her eyes pointing downwards. I knew at this point that she'd given up. Ian suggested at this point that if there was to be any hope for her survival she needed to have one of her back legs amputated, as it was starting to decay. She'd lost a lot of blood. A transfusion was ordered and on standby if required. Ian had to make a decision quickly; as he explained, Cody's pain was immense, and getting worse. It was time to see what was going on under the layer of dead skin - if decay had started to set in, it was unethical to keep her alive any longer. So, under sedation, Ian peeled back the dead skin. It proved to be our worst fear, decay had started and her organs were failing - there was no hope for her. I got the dreaded call for us to get there quickly and say our goodbyes - we were all outside when the phone rang. I was crying as I told Martin and the boys the news.

Justin walked away from me, crying. All we could do was wrap our arms around him. I felt awful that we'd put them through all this. If we'd known, she wouldn't make it we wouldn't have subjected them to daily visits, especially during the second week when she deteriorated so rapidly. Martin and I went to the vets. We didn't take Justin and Jake with us, we thought it would be too traumatic for them. Cody knew we were there, despite being heavily sedated. We said our goodbyes before watching her slip away - I can't even describe how horrendously hard this was.

For the same reason, to protect the boys, we kept as much of the investigation details from them as possible during that two-week period. When Jamie Downey and Andrew Stewart were identified and arrested, this was a very difficult time because we were dealing with our emotions and grieving after losing Cody.

It's all a bit of a blur; there were so many emotions. Having to console the boys and answer their many questions was very traumatic. We told them the two suspects' names and that they'd be arrested.

Jake had to go through the process of identifying the culprits in the police station. He was shown photos of the suspects, and others who looked similar - this was particularly harrowing for Jake. It turned out he couldn't identify them through the photos, even for an adult it's very difficult to identify someone amongst similar photos; it becomes very confusing. Without Jake's accurate description of the two men, the whole identification process would have been impossible. The CCTV footage, from the local pub, and the primary school, matched the description of the two men he'd relayed in such detail.

Martin and I had to deal with a lot of grief and anger when the culprits were caught. We were shown photos of the two suspects and it made our blood boil. An image in front of you makes it very real, and I found myself staring at them many times in disbelief that they could be capable of such a barbaric act of cruelty. Martin struggled with his emotions surrounding the whole attack, and still does today. I, instead, threw all my energy and focus towards getting justice, aiding the police investigation, and sharing any information we could find from the locals. We both spent a lot of time on Cody's site, giving updates and thinking of ways to continue fundraising and creating greater awareness of animal cruelty. This was the only way I could vent my pain, by trying to do everything in my power to make an example of this horrific crime and to hopefully prevent others from committing such cruel attacks.

I was determined we would get a prison sentence and refused to believe otherwise, despite only having circumstantial evidence. All odds were against us, but this determination was my driving force.

# CHAPTER FOUR: The Aftermath on Facebook

*We were understandably devastated when we saw Cody burnt, in pain, and visibly distressed. The two weeks between Cody's attack and her euthanasia were unbearable. Because all we could think about was Cody, we used Facebook to update family and friends on her condition. Word spread, however, and we received messages of support from people all over the world. I've included some of the posts here, to show how raw things felt at the time and how the fortnight unfolded.*

## 28 August 2012

Cody not great this morning. She's not eating again, but by lunchtime I brought her sausages and she ate one. Vet has told us this isn't going be a quick heal; her back legs are a big concern if the burns are very deep. Unfortunately, he won't know how bad it is until those bits of flesh come away. Thanks again for all your well-wishes, if only Cody knew how brilliant everyone has been.

**30 August 2012**

36,000 people. That is really unbelievable; so many great messages of support and hope. Thank you all very, very, much; we will continue to share pictures of Cody's recovery, but we have been told that she will get worse before she can get better. Thank you for all your kindness, donations towards our vets' bills and various products to help aid her recovery. Cody is being given the best care and I would really like to thank everyone at the vets in Moira. I brought the kids to see her today for the first time since her ordeal and it wasn't the easiest thing I've ever done. I don't want to talk about the scumbags who have done this, I just want Cody back safe and well. Thanks again, everyone.

**2 September 2012**

This time last week Cody was fine; if only I'd gotten up ten minutes earlier, none of this would have happened. It was my son's birthday yesterday and he got cards and presents, just like normal. He opened a card with £10 in it and without even thinking he said, "Give that to Cody". Heart-wrenching stuff.

**3 September 2012**

Cody's doing well today, eating, drinking and moving around. Steroids have given her a massive boost. Her skin has started to come away and some pinkness is showing (a good sign), and she's itchy (another good sign). The vets can't believe the change in her. Just reading your texts and emails - all the well-wishing must be working. Thank you all again.

**5 September 2012**

Cody is still doing well. She even played ball for a while. She's sporting a nice red coat after getting a bath earlier. Hoping for wee changes every day but I know it's going to take time. Thanks, everyone, for your continued support.

**8 September 2012**

It took a long while for the police investigator to very carefully and thoroughly build and strengthen this

case. The protocol and procedures he had to follow, step-by-step, meant leaving no stone unturned as he prepared an outline of the case to 'sell' to the PPS.
I want not only justice for Cody but to make a difference to all other animals; I want to fight for tougher sentencing for crimes of this nature. Martin and I were invited to attend a debate at Stormont to witness a plea for tougher sentencing; this was very interesting, and Cody's case was mentioned in great detail. We wanted to put pressure on any politician who could influence the justice minister into ensuring Cody's case made it to trial. We hope the culprits get a decent prison sentence and set a landmark for other animal abusers to do prison time. A year before Cody's attack the sentence was only six months for an animal cruelty case. This law was subsequently changed and the sentence increased to two years. Despite this, no one had received a prison sentence for animal cruelty; we wanted Cody's culprits to be the first, followed by any other cruelty cases. This debate and motion for even tougher sentencing was passed and we are still hoping and campaigning, waiting for the next stage

in this debate. I feel two years is not long enough; in America, a similar attack to Cody's would mean a sentence of ten years and hefty fines. The reason I want to continue campaigning is mainly because, as statistically proven, most notorious serial killers start off abusing and killing animals for pleasure before moving onto humans. There's a definite connection, so campaigning is very important to me. Cody's death will not be in vain, I want to make a difference to other animals. Cody will be the voice, now, and in the future, I hope.

At present, I'm campaigning not only for tougher sentences but for an animal offenders' list, similar to the sex offenders' list – a movement that will hopefully be called 'Cody's law'. This will ensure a record of animal abusers is kept and used to hopefully prevent possible future attacks. I would also like to campaign for more animal welfare officers, and for a policing system to be put in place, to keep a watchful eye on abusers banned from owning any animal. At present, there are no enforcing officers to keep a check on all this. I cannot ever come to terms with Cody's attack, which is why I have directed all my emotions into campaigning. I want to ensure Cody will always be remembered for making changes to laws that will hopefully protect other animals and preventing them from suffering the same fate.

**UPDATE**

Hello, just a quick update for you all. Cody's not very well tonight, she's really feeling the pain and her legs are in a bad way. This is going to be a long and hard fight, with many ups and downs. Hopefully, I'll have better news soon; again, thanks for all the support.

**9 September 2012**

Bad news. Cody didn't make it. She'd deteriorated from Friday and the vets tried everything they could. We're all gutted, but we know she was suffering and was only going to get worse.

**10 September 2012**

Lots of messages and emails to look at, I'll

get through them all in the next few days and reply to as many of you as possible. Thanks for all your support, it's been fantastic.

I'll put up some of the pictures and videos you've sent us; they're great, thank you all for taking the time to produce and share them with us.

Again, could I please ask if you could share and sign the e-petition and take a look at the 'Paws for Thought' web-page. If we all sign the petition, we could really make a difference. Thanks.

**12 September 2012**

I just want to thank everyone again for all the messages, gifts, donations and help. The kindness that has been shown to us can never be repaid and will never be forgotten. The vets in Moira were all brilliant in what must have been a very difficult situation, because of the public concern and media interest. They really looked after Cody and our family and told us every day how they became attached to her.

For James and Jennifer, who answered hundreds of emails and set everything up for us, we thank you. We hope you realise we couldn't have got through all this without you. To Tara Purdy and Vicky Wylie, who selflessly set up accounts to help pay for Cody's vet bills, again, we will always remember your kindness. Thanks to Sheelah Dale from Animal Connexions for all your help and messages of hope for Cody. Thank you to the people whose names we don't even know, who donated creams, rubs, blankets and doggie food. And to all of you who donated money towards Cody's vet bills through PayPal, even the kids who gave up their pocket money, we thank you all so very much. The first week, Facebook really did keep us sane, all the messages from the UK, and around the world, wishing Cody well. Many venting their anger at what she went through gave us hope in what was a sickening time.

But towards the end of the second week, we knew all was not going to be okay and Cody was really suffering. Thank you all so very much, I just hope you realise what you have given Cody and her family during the last few weeks with all your support and messages. We will never forget your kindness and, of course, our loving dog Cody.

**17 September 2012**

We got Cody's ashes back today from the vet, so a tough day coming for the kids. We also received your nice cards and messages that had been sent to the vets. All the gifts and cards for Cody from around the world have again touched our hearts. Thank you again.

**18 September 2012**

I recently put on a post about Cody's ashes being brought home. It may have upset some people that we had Cody cremated, especially after what she went through. Cody's ashes are sitting in our living room beside her Justice for Cody bag and hundreds of cards. We plan to have a day with our kids to say goodbye to Cody in our own way. The kids could not have been as involved as much if we'd buried her. We've also had the vet's and our integrity questioned as to when and why she was put to sleep. I can assure you all that Cody was given the best chance. 99.9% of Facebook understand how difficult this whole situation was for our family, but for the small minority, please think how my children would feel reading these hurtful comments.

**23 September 2012**

Hi, all, just an update on what we've been doing since we lost our beloved Cody. We're still trying very hard to come to terms with all this and we're missing Cody greatly; our home is just not the same without her. Small things like walking the kids to school each day are a daily reminder of our loss. We have been venting our anger and grief by focusing on organising a fundraiser in Cody's name for various animal charities - a day out for families and dogs alike. A day to hopefully meet you all and thank you for your support. We will, of course, keep you informed when we have more details. Meanwhile, can I please, please stress to everyone how important it is to sign the e-petition - we need tougher sentences for these inhumane, cruel acts.

## 26 September 2012

Hi, everyone. Last night was a success! We were kindly invited to Stormont to listen to a debate on cruelty to animals and tougher sentencing for these criminals. The motion was passed, which means progress, and that the issue is open for further discussion. This debate was sparked off by Cody's horrific act of cruelty at the hands of these grown men. We must all remember that there are many other forms of animal cruelty that have occurred and are still taking place today. This motion, on Cody's behalf, will hopefully benefit all animal cruelty cases and see justice dished out to the culprits. This debate will also hopefully encourage the current laws to actually be enforced. As of yet, there have been no convictions that have received the maximum penalty: two years in jail. The agricultural minister set these new laws, we just need to see them used. Steven Agnew (Green Party) also spoke about banning animal circuses. I've been very passionate about this since childhood and would like to appeal to you all to show your support too, as these animals are kept in appalling cramped conditions, and many subjected to violence just so that they perform for our enjoyment. I have taken care to explain to my children why I refuse to take them to these animal circuses.

We thank George Robinson (MLA), Paul Givan (MLA), Steven Agnew, and all others involved for inviting us along to the debate and giving such a passionate and justifiable discussion. We miss Cody so much, and hope and pray she will make a difference. We will continue to fight in her name.

**4 October 2012**

We are picking up our new puppy tomorrow. We are very excited but also overcome with sadness at the same time. We are missing Cody and know this is a new start but certainly not a replacement for her, there was only one Cody and we will never forget her lovely friendly and hyper ways! This new puppy will be very special though and will no doubt be over protected. We think it will help our boys and us have a new focus and help us through all this. This new pup was 1 of

8 collie pups found abandoned in a box in the Banbridge area, roughly around 7 weeks old. They are all in good health and lovely pups, hard to believe anyone could abandon them! So nice to get a rescue pup and will give him an extremely loving home. Also, we have confirmed Sat 24th November in the Stormont grounds there is going to be a fundraiser day in Cody's name. A day to hopefully meet you all and thank you for all your support. You can bring your dogs of course, and families along to enjoy a fun day. We have a few ideas and need to meet with the event's team of Steven Agnew (Green Party) and Assisi, who are organising this in Cody's name. Hopefully, we can make a change and help other animals in need so that Cody's tragic end to her short life can provide hope to make a real change. We've been asked a lot about the men who did this to Cody, all we can say is that it's in the police and the Justice system's hands, any questions should be asked to the P.S.N.I . Hope to see you all at the fundraiser. Natalie.

67,529 people reached

******************

We have decided on a name for our pup, the boys picked the name Rex. Cody and Rex are friends in Star Wars and this is their reason! Rex is so adorable, he is so affectionate and has really helped to brighten up our home again. Cody will always be missed though, we still struggle to cope with her horrific attack, it certainly isn't getting any easier to accept. In view of the fundraiser, we are having a meeting this week to discuss plans and will hopefully have more details by the end of the week. The leftover donations you all so kindly donated will be shared among various animal sanctuaries in Cody's name. We hope to help other animals, it will be at least some consolation to us after what our family have endured.

*Justin decided yesterday to look up the meaning of the name Codie. (This is the correct spelling of our Codie. I think I explained before that there was a mistake made when we had this site put up after Codie's attack!) Codie means "HELPER"! Justin couldn't wait to text me while I was working to tell me this and said I should share it with you all! How ironic after all Codie has done for animal welfare, animal sanctuaries/ charities and guide dogs! Truly amazing we think.*

## 8 October 2012

Hi everyone, sorry I haven't been commenting on this site for a while, I have had a beloved family member recently pass away. While I have been keeping an eye on things, my admin team have been helping out. I heard last Friday that a plea for an unfair trial was granted. I just want to ask you all, was it fair that our family pet Cody was taken, set alight with lighter fluid and left to suffer agonising pain for 2 weeks? Was it fair that my two children had to watch her suffer and slowly die? Did such a loving, trusting animal deserve this torture? Where is the fairness here? Please someone explains this to me as I would love an explanation.

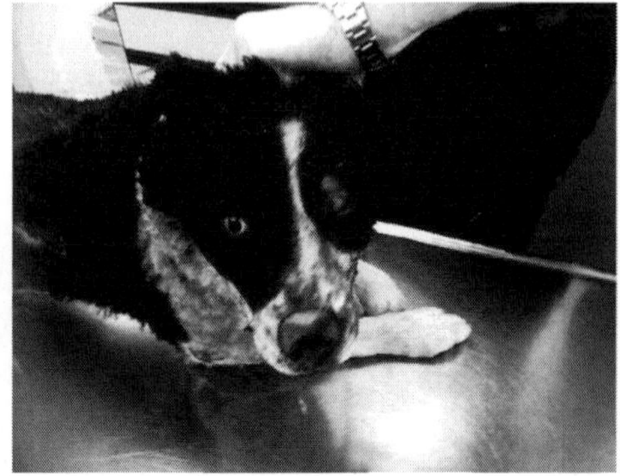

This surely is unfairness.

**4 May 2013**

This is what Jake, at seven years old, wrote a few days ago. It's not the type of story I have ever imagined him writing. It breaks our hearts having to read this; as you can see, while Rex has really helped, our boys will never forget Cody and what has happened.

***"Cody was the best dog ever. I took care of her, I played with her, and I loved her until two bad boys set her on fire and the vets had to put her to sleep. I never saw her again."***

**9th June 2013**

Hi everyone, just a wee update on our case. I picked up our petition, all put together in a thick booklet. It shows 10,500 plus signitures. I would like to thank Joe Kaminski and Alexandra Martin, from Chicago, for all their hard work putting this altogether with not only all the signitures and comments but a statement from us, saying how this has affected our family. Jake's letter, and a statement written by Joe and Alex on behalf of you all, expressing the reasons why justice must be served. This will help convince the PPS its definitely in the public interest to bring this to court. Also a big thankyou to Neil, a printer who helped put together this file, I know Neil didnt want any recognition for this, but we are truly grateful to him for offering his services so kindly. Most importantly we would like to thank all of you who signed the petition, without these signatures this would not have been possible, thankyou all so much. We will keep you posted on the case and thankyou for your continuing support.

**26 August 2013**

It's hard to believe it's now been a year since the attack. I've put off writing this post as it forces me to realise the true horrific nature of what actually happened. I try to blank it out most of the time because I don't know how to ever come to terms with it. I can't bear to think of the suffering and pain Cody so needlessly had to endure. You've all helped so much - I know you have felt our loss and pain too, and we, therefore, don't feel so alone in this. This year has been very hard on our family, and we're continually trying to deal with the daily troubles our boys experience. As time goes on it gets worse for them, between fears and anxiety are endless questions we can't answer. I feel their innocent minds have been corrupted and this will stay with them forever; this saddens us so much. Cody is either thought about or talked about every day in our house.

Cody's ashes still remain in a little wooden box on our windowsill, we intend to have a little burial service with our family maybe bury her under a tree and plant forget-me-nots. A lovely plaque made in memory a reminder of all the animals she has helped and will continue to do so.
Thank you all so much for sticking by us with your support, for all this time. It means so much to us.

**Messages from well-wishes by letter and cards**

Reading comforting words, some of which I've included, and from people we don't even know, proved a huge comfort to our family as we came to terms with the loss of Cody. Some people sent money for the boys to treat themselves while they were going through such a hard time, others sent cheques from collections they'd held on Cody's behalf. It's hard to put into words how touched we were by people's kindness, which was in stark contrast to the depravity and maliciousness shown by the two thugs who set Cody alight. The very best and worst of human nature, side by side.

*"Our hearts go out to you all as a family. Remember the good times, the things that made you all smile. You will all remember Cody as the darling dog she was. Cody is at peace now – others are not. I had a beautiful basset hound; he died suddenly, I think he was poisoned. I feel your heartache."*
***The Timoney family***

*"When we first heard the horrific news about little Cody we were all devastated. How anyone could hurt any animal, never mind a much-loved, beautiful dog like yours, is beyond us. As a family, we have three dogs, two being collies like Cody. If*

*anything happened to them it would be heart-breaking – dogs are on this planet much too short a time as it is.*

*We just wanted you to know that in the two sad weeks since those spineless individuals did that disgraceful thing to Cody she has touched the hearts of thousands of people. Your little dog's memory will not only live on in the hearts of her loving family, but also in the hearts of all those that waited for news of her progress each day, and who willed her to get better again. She was a brave little thing and it's awful that her fight and pain became too much for her.*

*We hope that you have good memories of Cody and that justice is handed out to those who did what they did on that terrible Sunday. It's very true what they say about dogs leaving their footprints on your heart forever.*

*Sleep tight, little Cody."*
***The Simpson family***

*"My 88-year-old aunt's house was attacked in July, flammable liquid poured*

*through her letterbox and her home ignited. She, like the rest of us, was so vexed about what happened to Cody. Yes, there are some terrible people out there, but thankfully they are outnumbered by the many decent people that exist.*
*We also share your distress; we know what it's like to lose a much-loved pet in the most tragic of circumstances. Our cat, Ginger, was torn apart by two unsupervised Staffordshire bull terriers and like Cody, was eventually put out of his misery by the vet. You will never get over what happened to Cody, like we never got over what happened to Ginger, but believe me, you will move on and, in time, like us, give a loving home to another animal that I'm sure will be spoilt rotten."*
***The Major family***

*"Our prayers are with you all at such a devastating time in your lives. How can people be so cruel to such a lovely wee dog? Our dog, Mick, was attacked with a tennis racket while with our son, by a grown man. He made a complete recovery, but it took us a long time to get over it."*
***The McCloskey family***

*"Enclosed is a cheque, which is money I collected for Cody's vet bills the week after her attack. I was still trying to collect more when she sadly passed away.*

*I can't begin to imagine what your family has been through with this tragedy. I was devastated that Cody didn't make it. I cried many tears for her and your family – and I don't even know you. Every time I looked at my wee dog I kept thinking, 'What if it had been her?' I can't imagine the pain you're feeling."*
***Kirsty***

With the donations received from people across the world, we felt we could turn Cody's terrible ordeal into something positive. With the money donated we managed to pay Cody's vet fees. Made donations to various local animal sanctuaries where we did a cheque presentation at out Stormont event to these charities. The Stormont event was another reason to raise more money and awareness. We arranged for various politicians to come along and speak on behalf of all animals. Steven Agnew, from the Green Party, sponsored this event and through the 'Justice for Cody' site all supporters came together and helped out. There were offers of all sorts of equipment including; public portable toilets, a stage, stage equipment, etc. There was a lot of organising that went into all this and I'd never done anything like it before!

The event enabled various animal charities to set up stalls where they sold Cody merchandise which we had bought with the leftover donation money. We purchased Cody wristbands and Justice for Cody bags for life. A supporter, Karen Houston, inspired us after she beautifully hand painted a hessian bag for life with a lovely portrait of Cody and a Justice for Cody logo which she donated to us as a gift. This inspired us to print more bags similar to these, and donate them to various animal charities to sell and keep the profits; also it would be a great legacy to Cody. People attending the event were donating to charity buckets, buying the merchandise, and also brought along food and blankets for these charities. Altogether around £30,000 was raised. This included the initial donation funds and profits made from the various animal charities through the merchandise sales and bucket collections. There was also the £5000 we raised for the guide dogs for the blind to name a guide dog puppy CODY.

# Cody in happier times

# After the attack *(taken at the vets)*

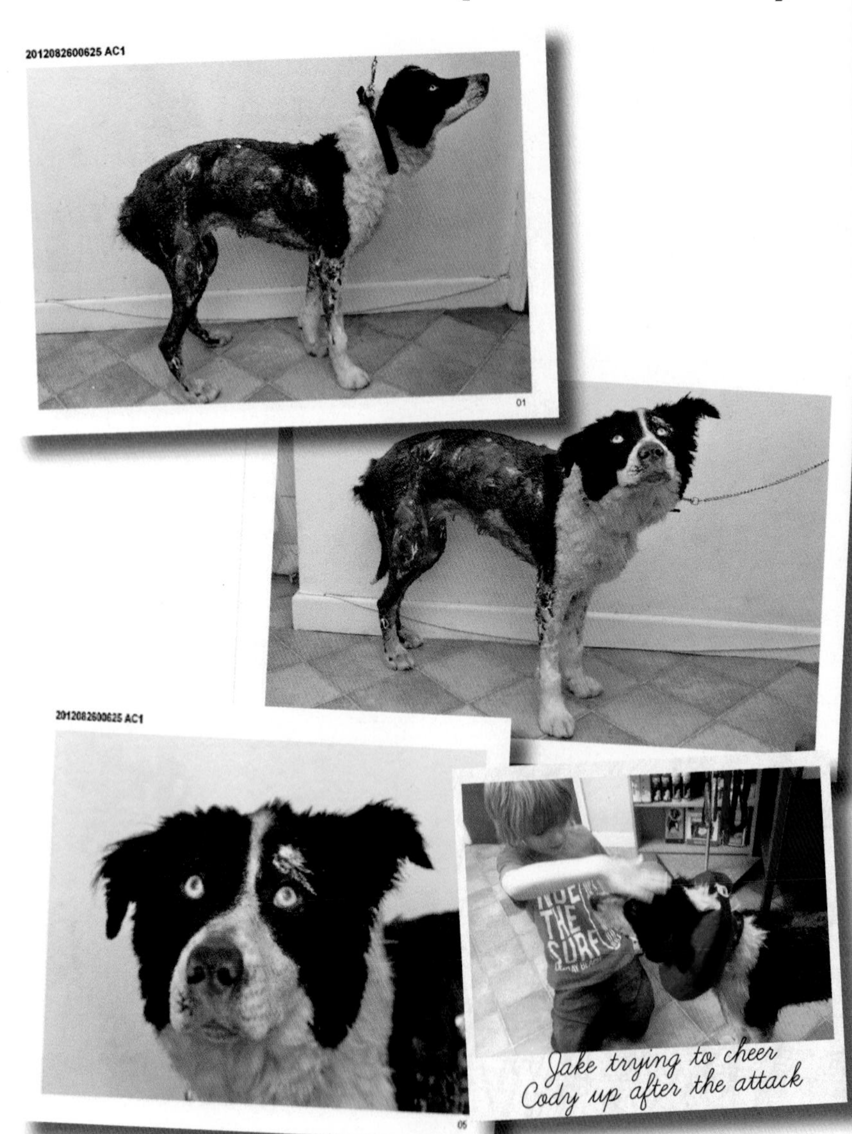


Jake trying to cheer Cody up after the attack

# Cody Remembered

## The Campaign against Animal Cruelty ... and campaigning for Cody's Law

# Fundraising in Cody's Name

# Miscellaneous Really Important Stuff

Codie was the best dog ever I took
care of her I played with her
and I loved her until two bad boys
set her on fire and the vets had to
put her to sleep and I never saw
her agan

# The Family Coming to Terms... with Rex & CJ

# We Miss You Cody...

## CHAPTER FIVE: The Trial

The duration of the trial was a very stressful experience. With every court date, I was a bundle of nerves, waiting to hear if it would continue to the next stage. I had a lot of other stress in my life – as the trial unfolded my step-mum was terminally ill. She passed away in June 2014, before the sentencing. Justin's health had also been an ongoing battle of medical tests throughout the previous four years. The strain and pressure I felt as the trial played out was immense.

There were more than a few occasions when I thought we'd lose the case. A particular trial date sticks out in my mind was when the defence team made a plea for the court venue to be moved from Craigavon Crown Court to Belfast Crown Court, on the grounds of an unfair trial. The date of the plea was the same day as my step-mum's funeral. I was already very emotional and grieving; when I heard the news I broke down and then became overwhelmingly angry. I couldn't get the word 'unfair' out of my mind; these culprits had the cheek to say it was an unfair venue for the court, because it was possible that members of the jury may know them and know about the case. I couldn't believe that the judge granted this 'unfair'. Was what they did to Cody *fair*?

This move eventually proved to be to our advantage. At Belfast, we got a fantastic judge, who was also a dog behavioural expert and collie owner. He was clearly disgusted and appalled by this crime, therefore, gave the maximum penalty he possibly could. Each stage of the trial was very stressful, highlighted every step of the way by the press. Everyone was talking about it wherever we went; Justin and Jake undoubtedly heard many harrowing details as we talked to various people and to the press. Jake suffered greatly each time Cody's case was in the eye of the media - any progress with his counsellor quickly reversed and his distress showed in his behaviour and personality again and again. At these points, we had to arrange more counselling for him, which caused me a lot of anger. The ongoing trauma the attack caused my two boys at such a young age was cruel and unnecessary.

I found the time between the trial and the sentencing very tough. It was crucial to us; all the work, energy and time we'd put into fighting for justice lay in the hands of a jury and judge. I couldn't even allow myself to think that the perpetrators wouldn't get a prison sentence; I just hoped and prayed justice would be served.

There was no doubt Cody's attack, suffering and subsequent death hit a nerve with people, infuriating and disgusting them in equal measure. By the time Andrew Stewart and Jamie Downey's preliminary hearing came, the campaign had received a lot of media coverage.

As the hearing began, an individual, believed to be a member of Jamie Downey's family, released what was thought at the time to be pepper spray inside the court. Jamie's immediate reaction to the court reporter was, "Sorry, I just farted." He and other family members quickly left the courtroom.

His attempt to scare the Cody supporters was followed by further intimidation outside court. Mirroring practices by

Northern Irish Paramilitary, he verbally attacked supporters and a press photographer at the scene then took photographs of their car registration plates suggesting, "I'll get you."

After the incident, a chemical detection team was sent into the courtroom, who confirmed the substance released was not pepper spray but more likely to have been a liquid cartridge from an electronic cigarette. In its concentrated form, and without a filter, this carries no risk of long-term effects; however, Cody's supporters suffered headaches and a persistent cough throughout the following week.

***The following newspaper excerpts show how the court case and surrounding events continued to unfold...***

"Two men accused of burning a Co Antrim family's dog to death are set to argue for the charges against them to be thrown out of court.

Martin and Natalie Agnew's three-year-old border collie, Cody, was attacked last summer close to their home in Moira.

Yesterday, solicitors for Jamie Downey and Andrew Richard Stewart, both 22, told Lisburn Magistrates Court they would be making 'no case to answer' applications. If granted, this would mean the end of the case in connection with the dog's death.

Downey and Stewart are accused of causing suffering to Cody on August 26, 2012. They had been due to be connected to that charge yesterday and a preliminary enquiry held, potentially committing them to the Crown Court for trial, but both were adjourned in light of future defence submissions.

District Judge Rosemary Watters granted legal aid to both Downey and Stewart and adjourned the case for two weeks to hear submissions on the 'no' case.

Under the Welfare of Animals Act (Northern Ireland) a person found guilty of unnecessary suffering can be sentenced to a maximum prison term of two years, a fine, or both.

In an incident that shocked and horrified animal lovers across Northern Ireland, three-year-old Cody suffered horrific burns to most of her body when she was doused in petrol and set on fire in the Maghaberry Road area of Moira.

A statement issued on behalf of the family at the time said they had been left gutted by Cody's death, but they knew 'she was suffering and it was only going to get even worse'."
***Belfast Telegraph***

"A man who admitted setting fire to a family's pet dog has been told he will face an inevitable prison sentence.
Cody, a three-year-old collie, had been so badly burned her ribs were visible through the charred flesh. She survived for two weeks but had to be put down.

Stewart, who had denied the charges for two years, dramatically changed his plea minutes before the dog's owners were due to give evidence.

Judge David McFarland said: "It is a

serious matter. You will be facing an inevitable prison sentence."

The judge also requested that a psychiatric assessment be carried out on the defendant to try and understand why he carried out the attack. Judge McFarland then told the jury of seven women and five men he would be directing them to find the defendant guilty.
His co-accused, Jamie Downey, 23, from Chestnut Hall Avenue, also in Moira, admitted a single charge of perverting the course of justice, while the animal cruelty charges were left on the court's books.
The trial had earlier heard Stewart and Downey had repeatedly lied about their whereabouts on the morning Cody was attacked. They had attended a house party close to the dog's family home and were identified by eyewitnesses walking along railway tracks towards a quarry on the outskirts of Maghaberry, accompanied by a black and white dog."
***www.newsletter.co.uk***

"A source close to the case told Sunday Life: "As they continued walking, the dog was still following them along a railway track. They said they couldn't shake her off and she wouldn't go home. When they reached a quarry, Downey told Stewart that he needed to go to the toilet.

As he stood urinating with his back to Stewart, he heard a noise and turned around to see Stewart pouring flammable liquid on the dog and setting her alight. Downey said to Stewart: "What the f**k did you do that for?" and Stewart is said to have replied: "I don't know. I just felt like it."

Stewart just did it out of pure badness. The dog didn't bite them or anything. It just went for a walk with them.

Police and prosecutors say it was a totally unwarranted attack on a defenceless and harmless three-year-old collie dog.

The pair fled the scene, but observant residents in the area had seen them on a drunken prowl from early morning.

Instead of Downey going to the police or Cody's family to tell them the truth, he decided to cover up for his friend and frustrate the PSNI investigation by giving false information.

Animal rights activists are staging a protest at Belfast Crown Court when Stewart and Downey are sentenced."
***Sunday Life***

"Cody's owners called for the maximum sentence of two years' imprisonment to be enforced as it became clear that one of the two men who admitted the deliberate attack would face time in jail.

Natalie Agnew said: "We will try and have this extended if possible. We hope that this makes a statement to the people out there who would abuse animals – it's not acceptable and you will be punished. We want to speak on behalf of all other abused animals out there, not just for Cody, so that she didn't die in vain."

Stewart and Downey were both released on bail and ordered to come back before the court for sentencing. It is understood that Stewart's prison sentence will be the first given for an attack on animals since the Welfare of Animals Act (Northern Ireland) 2011 came into effect in 2012.

News of the intended sentencing was welcomed by the Ulster Society for the Prevention of Cruelty to Animals (USPCA). Spokesman David Wilson said: "The USPCA are delighted that a custodial sentence will be handed down in this case of this premeditated callous act of cruelty to an animal. We're hoping that the accused will receive a significant sentence of the maximum two years that can be handed down, and that it acts as a deterrent to anyone else who would deliberately seek to hurt an animal."

Mrs Agnew said: "We won't really have closure until we get the sentence and we see Andrew Stewart going to prison. It may all hit me then and I will need to deal with it."

She said that the family hoped to bury Cody's ashes under a tree on their land and would sow forget-me-not seeds over the top of her grave.
***Belfast Telegraph***

"He was only a child of six when two evil men came into his life and turned it upside down.

Jake Agnew found out just how bad some big boys could be the day Andrew Stewart and Jamie Downey decided to set Cody, the little boy's much-loved three-year-old pet, alight.

"Jake blamed what had happened on himself, for a long time, for about a year afterwards, because he had seen Cody in the back garden earlier that morning," his mother said. "Just after that he went upstairs and had noticed the two boys walking down. He kept saying over and over to himself, 'If I had brought Cody in, then it wouldn't have happened.' He began to hate himself. He would look at himself in the mirror and think he was ugly and ask how anyone could like him.

No matter what we said, he wouldn't change his mind. His whole personality changed, but the counselling has really helped and we might still have to have it again after the sentencing."

Now aged nine, the young boy had to be prepared for giving evidence in court, but thankfully was spared that ordeal because of the guilty pleas. Mrs Agnew and her husband Martin have focused their attention on ensuring that their sons Justin, 12, and Jake cope as well as possible with the aftermath of the traumatic incident.

"Justin has had nightmares ever since and is afraid of being on his own," added Mrs Agnew. "Until you go through a situation like this, you don't realise the effect it can have, particularly the long-term effect it has had on them and the problems we're still dealing with.""
***Belfast Telegraph***

"Standing in the dock, Stewart stared straight ahead as almost eighty 'Justice for Cody' supporters filed into the public gallery behind him. While they remained dignified and silent the tension in the courtroom heightened as his co-defendant, Jamie Downey appeared in Court 12 of Laganside Courts thirty minutes later.

After Judge McFarland had spent a further ten minutes considering sentencing, he recalled the horrors the little dog had suffered and the effects on her heartbroken family.

Without taking his eyes off the judge, Stewart's face flushed as he heard he would be living a few miles from his family home in Maghaberry's high-security jail with rapists and murderers for ten months – and then a further ten months on licence.

His pal, Jamie Downey, stood in the dock with him to hear his fate. Downey was charged with perverting the course of justice and was jailed for six months. A charge of animal cruelty was left on the books.

Judge McFarland described Stewart's attack on Cody as evil, vile and beyond comprehension. He said: "This was a particularly appalling act. Cody was a much-loved pet, having lived with the Agnew family since she was a puppy. Domesticated animals do not have the in-built safety features of feral creatures that rely on fear and flight to protect them against predators. If properly reared and trained - and Cody was - it will not see humans as predators but will instead adopt a friendly disposition.

It is very hard to fathom any rational motivation for Stewart's conduct. He was 21, had a reasonable education, a good upbringing in a stable family, had to all intents and purposes a clear criminal record, and also a good work record.

Once he had committed the act and realised the enormity of his conduct and the resulting injuries to the dog, he simply walked away, leaving the dog to make its own way home, rendering no assistance. This conduct raises fears that other vulnerable creatures would be at risk in his company. Saying it was a moment of madness is not an adequate explanation.

I order that Stewart be disqualified from owning or keeping any animal for a period of thirty years. He may not apply to terminate his disqualification before the end of twenty years. I also order him to pay compensation to Martin and Natalie to cover veterinary expenses. I have every confidence they will donate any amount of compensation received to a suitable canine, or other animal, charity.

David Wilson from the USPCA welcomed Stewart's sentence but said a register must be set up to monitor people banned from keeping animals. He said: "A prison sentence sends out the right message, but if the courts are going to hand out bans there must be an effective way of ensuring those people don't just go out and get themselves a pet."

PSNI chief inspector Jonathan Wilson said: "As a nation of animal lovers, we see our pets as family members. It's only right that those found responsible for this sickening attack were brought to justice and, as a result, have been punished."
***Daily Mirror***

Outside the court, Mrs Agnew expressed relief and said she believed justice had been done.
She said: "We are delighted with the outcome today. We have waited two years

for the guilty verdict and we look forward to the sentencing."

Mrs Agnew described the previous two years as horrendous. "The effect this has had on the children is still ongoing, let alone what they actually did to the poor dog."

Mr Agnew said Cody had been almost unrecognisable because of the extent of her injuries. "The first time I saw Cody when she came back I didn't recognise her, it was that bad," he said. "I will never forget the smell or what she looked like."
***The Irish News***

"A twisted thug who set fire and killed Cody the dog made jokes about pouring petrol on himself just moments after admitting the crime in court.

Andrew Stewart finally pleaded guilty to animal cruelty on Thursday after torturing the three-year-old collie whose horrific story made headlines across the UK.
The remorseless pet killer is living in fear of being attacked after the UDA made

veiled threats against him. Just minutes after walking out of Belfast Crown Court, where his trial was due to go into its second day, the 23-year-old posted sickening references to what he did.

Stewart, who had not posted anything on his Facebook page since being charged two years previously, took to the social networking site minutes after pleading guilty. And instead of taking the opportunity to apologise publicly for his terrible crime, he made light of what he'd done.

He posted: "Anyone got a light? Spilt petrol on myself.....#scumbagforlife." The comments fanned the flames of hate against the dog killer and the UDA-linked south Belfast UPRG posted ominous comments about Stewart's.

The UPRG stated: "Local reps have been contacted by residents of the Derriaghy area over their concern about the presence of the now convicted Dog Killer from Maghaberry, Mr Stewart. There are some very high feelings about in the community regarding this, and it would probably be very wise of him to be careful where he frequents for his own safety."

And comments made about that statement were even more threatening. One member of the public wrote: "Just cut the ba***rd from ear to ear then pour flammable liquid over him and set him on fire..."

Last night, a loyalist source from South Belfast told the Sunday World that people were treating Stewart as if he was a sex offender. "He is hated for what he did," said the source. "Feelings are running very high because what he did was just so terrible. They are viewing him on a par with sex offenders. The fact he's been making jokes about it has only made things worse. If he'd thrown his hands up and said sorry straightaway, he might have been okay, but it's the fact that he clearly doesn't give a s**t."
***Sunday World***

"The judge rejected claims Stewart was sorry. He said: "In this case there has been no remorse. In my view, the recent expressions of regret are merely evidence

of self-pity. The plea was very late, and the change of mind only followed when Downey had indicated to his counsel that he was now prepared to tell the truth."
***The Ulster Star***

"Two thugs involved in setting fire to a defenceless dog were handed more than £16,000 from the taxpayer as they tried to escape justice.

Andrew Stewart and Jamie Downey were jailed last month over their roles in the death of Cody, the dog. The attack sparked outrage across Northern Ireland.

It has emerged that Stewart and Downey – who denied their guilt for two years – were each handed £8,000 in legal aid to fund their defence. The total legal aid bill for the case was £16,734. The figure was released by Justice Minister David Ford following an Assembly question from DUP MLA Lord Morrow.

Cody's owner, Natalie Agnew, said she was angered by the cost. "It is disgusting that taxpayers have been left to foot the bill for

Cody's killers," she said. "It's a real shock; it's a disgrace, because they knew for two years and allowed the case to drag on. All the time others were paying for it."
***Belfast Telegraph***

# CHAPTER SIX: What The Judge Had To Say

*The following comes from the closing statements in the Court when summarising the case and passing the sentences. Some of the points have been covered in snippets within the newspaper articles above, but we felt it important to show all the final closing words in full and in context.*

"Cody was a much-loved pet, having lived with the Agnew family since she was a puppy. The dog had attached itself to the defendants that morning. Domesticated animals do not have the inbuilt safety features of feral creatures which rely on fear and flight to protect them against predators. The domesticated canine now sees its adopted human family as its pack and will assume its role within the pack structure being subservient to the human pack leader. If properly reared and trained, and clearly Cody was, it will not see other humans as predators, but instead will adopt a friendly disposition in the company of humans, including strangers.

Instead of taking care of Cody and returning her to her owners, Stewart savagely attacked her in the most evil and vile fashion. It is beyond comprehension that any human being could act in such a manner towards any defenceless creature, which was posing no threat to him. It is very hard to fathom any rational motivation for Stewart's conduct. He was 21 years of age, had a reasonable education, a good upbringing in a stable family, and had to all intents and purposes a clear criminal record, with a good work record. Whatever that motivation, once he had committed the act and realised the enormity of his conduct and the resulting injuries to the dog, he simply walked away, leaving the dog to make its own way home, rendering no assistance whatsoever. Conduct of this type does raise fears within the court's mind that other vulnerable living creatures, be they animal or human, would be at risk in his company. The absence of any psychosis, personality disorder or mood disorder (according to Dr Loughret, consultant psychiatrist) is reassuring at one level, yet disturbing in that it offers no explanation for his conduct.

I am taking into account the anguish that has been suffered by the Agnew family. This was a well-structured family, living what would appear to be a normal happy family life in a quiet village in rural Northern Ireland. The parents and the two boys had a much-loved pet, which was so cruelly taken from them. They had to suffer the anguish of seeing their dog with these serious injuries, of living through the attempted rehabilitative treatment, and then the parents had to come to the decision to end Cody's life, in circumstances which were not of their making or choosing. A decision to euthanize is very often the final act of kindness that an owner can render to his or her pet dog. It may arise as a result of old age, illness or unforeseen traumatic injury. It should never fall on any owner to make a decision that the Agnew family had to make. Subsequent to that decision, there has followed a period of two years of having to lie, and re-live the events and finally the preparation for the trail, which would have necessitated both Natalie and young Jake having to give evidence. For the parents, they have had the unenviable task of having to explain to their two young sons how this could have happened – why any human being would do such a thing to an animal, particularly their beloved family pet. Each member of the family, in their own way, has spoken in very moving terms about how this event has impacted upon them and their family. For cases of animal cruelty, there are no sentencing guidelines from the Court of Appeal. The maximum sentence is 2 year's imprisonment. Recently the Sentencing Council in Norther Ireland has approved some guidance to the Magistrates' Court, where the maximum sentence is 6 month's imprisonment. The actual starting points and range of sentences are of little relevance, but they do set out important aggravating features in cases of this type and of particular relevance, in this case, is the fact that gratuitous violence was used by dousing the coat with an inflammable liquid and then igniting it. A further aggravating factor is the impact that the offending has had on the Agnew family, and particularly the younger members of the family.

In mitigation I take into account Stewart's age – he was 21 and had a virtually clear criminal record. He did enter a plea of guilty, although it was on the second day of the trial. It is normal for courts to recognise a plea of guilty by reducing the sentence. Courts do this as the plea is an acknowledgment of guilt and as such may display remorse, it can avoid witnesses from giving evidence, and may avoid costs and expenses associated with the running of a contested trial. The later the plea, the less credit is given. In this case, there has been no remorse. In my view, the recent expressions of regret are merely evidence of self-pity. The plea was very late, and the change of mind only followed when Downey had indicated to his counsel that he was now prepared to tell the truth. The only positive aspects flowing from the late plea were that Natalie Agnew and Jake Agnew were not required to give evidence and that some time and costs have been saved.

I am aware that there has been extensive interest, in this case, as the plight of this dog, and its owners, have touched the hearts of many in Northern Ireland and further afield. There have been calls for the maximum sentence of 2 years to be imposed. Lawton LJ in the case of **R-v-Amber and Hargreaves (unreported) 24th November 1975** explained how judges should approach sentences falling into the higher category of cupability. He said, *"It is, of course, a principle in sentencing that maximum sentences should only be passed for the worst kind of offence. But it is to be borne in mind that when judges are asking themselves whether they should pass the maximum sentence, they should not use their imagination to conjure up unlikely worst possible kinds of case. What they should consider is the worst type of offence which comes before the court within the broad band of that type. Where the maximum sentence is low, the band may be wide."*

Although this case is of some vintage, the principle has been recently endorsed in the cases of **R-v-Butt (2006) 2 Cr App R (s) 364** and **R-v-Bright (2208) EWCA Crim 462** In **Bright** Judge LJ stated at (29) – *"The maximum sentence permitted by statute is reserved not for the worst possible case which can realistically be* *conceived, but for cases which in the statutory context are truly identified as cases of the utmost gravity."*

I am aware that this case falls into the band where the maximum should be imposed, but for mitigating factors. Had this case gone to verdict, the appropriate sentence taking into account Stewart's age and lack of criminal record would have been 22 months. Early acknowledgment of guilt followed by a guilty plea would have resulted in a reduction of one-third – over seven months. The late plea and the circumstances surrounding it will only attract 2 months' reduction so the sentence will be 20 month's imprisonment. As required by Article 8 of the Criminal Justice (NI) Order 2008, I specify that the licence period shall be 10 months. I recommend to the Department of Justice that it considers the Probation Officer's suggested condition in relation to the Managing Alcohol Programme.

I order that Stewart be disqualified under Article 33 of the 2011 Act from owning or keeping any animal for a period of 30 years. He may not apply to terminate this disqualification before the end of 20 years. I also order Stewart to pay compensation of £2,600 to Martin and Natalie Agnew to cover the cost of veterinary expenses. I understand that some of these costs may already have been defrayed by funds contributed by well-wishers. If that is the case, re-imbursement to the donors is likely an impossible task, but I have every confidence that Mr and Mrs Agnew will donate any amount of compensation received to a suitable canine or other animal charity. I take into account his current financial position and his earning capacity after his release. I acknowledge that courts should be slow to impose immediate custodial sentences and large compensation orders at the same time. Bearing this in mind, I propose to allow Stewart to pay the amount in instalments of £100 per month, the first instalment being due on the 1st June 2016. This will allow him sufficient time after his release from prison to have the ability to pay the amount. It is important that he, and others, realise that there is very often a financial consequence to their criminal activity. There will also be an Offender Levy of £25.

Downey, has pleaded guilty to a different offence – doing an act of perverting the course of justice. It is acknowledged by the prosecution that although he had originally been charged with the offence of animal cruelty, he had nothing to do with the actual attack on the dog. He had been in the company of Stewart and would have been aware that Cody had attached herself to the pair of youths. He would have been aware that Stewart had attacked the dog, yet despite this, he remained in the company of Stewart, he did nothing to alleviate the suffering of Cody knowing that she had been injured in a most grievous fashion, and then through some misguided loyalty to Stewart agreed with him to concoct what were false stories to divert police attention away from both defendants. No-one is ever punished for the company they keep and the friendships they maintain, but I have to say Downey did show extremely poor judgement in promoting his friendship with Stewart, knowing the conduct that Stewart was capable of, over the interests of the innocent Agnew family and the community in general.

Perverting the course of justice carries a potential life sentence, but it covers a very wide range of conduct. Courts will be concerned with motivation on the part of the offender, the impact that the conduct has on others, and on the institutions of the state. This conduct in providing a false account to police, did not interfere with the police investigation to a large extent, primarily as it would have been perceived by the police as a lying account from an early stage, however during that early period it had the potential to point the finger of suspicion towards other, innocent, parties. It did however mean that the police were required to carry out extensive enquiries to seek out and accumulate evidence to establish Stewart's guilt. This in turn would have added to the cost of the investigation, and the time taken obviously added to the frustration and anguish of the Agnew family.

In mitigation I take into account his age – he was 21 years of age – and his clear record. He has a good work ethic, and has been supported by references which speak highly of the positive aspects of his character. He entered his plea at the first opportunity. It is clear that driven by his conscience, he eventually decided to tell the truth, and thus end the Agnew's nightmare. His conduct forced Stewart to change his plea, a course Stewart is unlikely to have taken in the normal course of events.

A full and frank disclosure at the time of the original crime would have avoided the period of delay resulting from the police investigation and the trial process. It emboldened Stewart to think that if he kept to his story he might evade justice, and it led to extending the period of the Agnew's grief and anguish, delaying this moment of sentencing and if not closure for them, the end of this sad chapter in their lives.

The sentence, after a trial would have been 9 months custody, and will be reduced to 6 months to take into account your plea of guilty. There will also be an Offender levy of £25.

## Chapter Seven: A Political Perspective to Animal Cruelty

In late August 2012, I sat down with my family to watch the evening news and was both horrified and saddened by the horrific story of the terrible cruelty inflicted on a family pet which had been doused with a flammable liquid and set alight.

As an animal lover and a parent, I was shocked that such a mindless act of cruelty could be perpetrated on an innocent family pet. I could see the pain and anguish the Agnew family were suffering.

At this stage of the story, I did not realise that this awful act of cruelty would mark a sea change in attitudes towards animal welfare in Northern Ireland. Nor did anyone realise how it would galvanise a community of animal lovers to come together, step up and publically demand that abusers are held accountable by the legal system.

It was an ordinary family caught in

extraordinary circumstances; who were struggling with both the experience of losing a much-loved family pet and the media attention that inevitably followed. As a father with two young children of my own, I didn't know how I was going to explain such a random act of cruelty to my own kids and protect them from the potential psychological damage.

As a politician and as Leader of the Green Party in Northern Ireland, animal rights and animal welfare are personally very important to me and many of my Party colleagues. My passion for animal rights predates my involvement in formal politics. I am proud to have carried those values forward into my role as an MLA and for putting animal issues on the agenda before it had become fashionable to do so. I am delighted that animal welfare is beginning to be taken seriously by the political class.

Because of the volatile political situation that existed in Northern Ireland, animal welfare has sadly been neglected for decades. Other more pressing issues dominated the political and media agenda, and there was little space to expose, discuss or deal with animal welfare issues. Thankfully, the signing of the Good Friday Agreement in 1998 began the 'normalisation' of politics.

Political leaders now find themselves more accountable and must be more responsive to the needs and requests of their voters. The Green Party has always prioritised protecting the most vulnerable in our society. It is the core of our political beliefs that we provide a voice for those, including animals, who can't speak for themselves. We have always been true to those convictions and our presence in the local Northern Ireland Assembly since 2011 means that animal welfare is being kept on the political agenda.

In 2010, we brought forward the Hunting Bill to the Assembly which would have brought Northern Ireland into line with the rest of the UK by banning the hunting of wild animals with dogs. This is the only region of the UK where such barbaric practices as fox and stag hunting with hounds are legally permitted.

While some individual MLAs supported the ban, sadly, the proposal failed as no other political party gave the Bill it's backing. At the time of writing, I am in the process of trying to bring forward a motion to call for a ban so that the Assembly can debate this once again.

I anticipate getting more support this time. Unfortunately not because members of the Assembly have had been enlightened, but because sometimes democracy works. Increasingly, people in Northern Ireland are lobbying their politicians on animal issues. There is now greater awareness of the cruelty, not just to the fox or the stag, but to dogs as well.

The politicians know that their response could make the difference at the next election. The Green Party in Northern Ireland will continue to challenge those who still justify this horrific activity. We will continue to challenge the myths used by those who condone hunting; the fact still remains that animals are sentient beings which feel fear and pain. We cannot allow hunting to continue as a legitimate activity in a civilised society.

The Green Party condemns the hunting down of an animal, with all the terror that animal will experience, for it then to either be ripped apart by dogs or summarily killed by a huntsman. Where is the 'sport' in this situation? Suffering and cruelty have no place in any activity described as a sport.

**Cruelty to animals under any circumstances is simply not acceptable.**

The tragedy of Cody's horrible death and the naked cruelty so vividly exposed in news reports was a catalyst for bringing animal welfare to the forefront of the agenda in Northern Ireland.

If there is any small comfort to be drawn from the experience of Cody and the Agnew family, it is that this terrible experience galvanised public and political opinion that animal welfare matters. Many people from diverse backgrounds, and from a wide geographical spread, rallied on social media to support the Agnew family at the time of the attack. They were moved by the horrific pictures of the suffering inflicted on an innocent family pet and the terrible ramifications for the family involved.

Many of those people have stayed in touch with the family and each other and a network of animal welfare activism has grown organically. A key aspect of the subsequent campaigning has been for justice to be done in cases of animal cruelty.

In the fallout from that terrible incident, we saw the worst of people in those who inflicted the suffering and the best of people in those who stepped up and offered their support and help. Within a few days of Cody's death, over 70,000 people had signed up to the Facebook campaign. Thousands of pounds in personal donations had been offered, and many strong feelings had been expressed in those social media posts.

Sadly, Cody could not survive her injuries despite the tens of thousands of people rooting for her and there was a collective howl of anger and pain when she died. In the middle of this maelstrom of anger and sadness were the Agnew family still struggling to come to terms with a tragedy that had come out of the blue and had inflicted a lifelong scar on them. I knew that I was in a privileged position as a politician, as I am used to dealing with public demands and the media spotlight, but for those who are new to it this process can be daunting and intimidating.

Naturally, in the wake of Cody's death, there was a lot of anger and sorrow. The family and their supporters felt lost, and they needed something positive to channel their energy into. Having been approached by the Agnews, who were aware of the Green Party's commitment to animal causes, my team and I organised a public rally to put animal rights into the spotlight.

The idea was to harness the positive energy which had emerged from a tragic situation. I also wanted to give the Agnews something very practical to focus on, so the rally also became a fundraising event for a number of animal welfare charities including Guide Dogs. I had worked with many of these organisations in the past in terms of raising awareness and pushing for tougher legislation. I felt it was important to create a space where people could express their feelings, show solidarity and most importantly channel their energy into something positive and life affirming.

My job as an elected Member of the Legislative Assembly (MLA) affords me the ability to stage events at our local Parliament Buildings known as the Stormont Estate. So I met with the Agnew family and talked through ideas for the event that was organised for Saturday November 24, 2012.

Despite freezing weather conditions, hundreds of people (and their dogs, of course!) came to the rally to show their support. They donated money to the animal charities represented on the day including The Dogs' Trust, Assisi Animal Sanctuary and Guide Dogs. It brought the message loud and clear to the front door of government that this issue need to be taken seriously.

But perhaps the most poignant legacy of the rally is the fact that enough money was raised to start the training of a guide dog which was named in Cody's memory. I was so moved to see the two young Agnew boys moving through the crowd with their collection buckets that bore a picture of their beloved pet cruelly snatched away from them.

I saw how the crowd reacted to them and how they were literally engulfed by kindness, love and support of the thousands of animal-loving citizens who stood in the freezing cold for two hours to support them. The Agnews drew on their inner strength and led from the front in terms of positivity, and that allowed the mass of people supporting them to do the same.

Animal welfare is something I truly believe that we need to take seriously in our society, and the infliction of cruelty towards animals remains a major injustice and is one in which we are all obligated to tackle. This incident further galvanised me to push Ministers in Government to look at the issue of animal welfare in Northern Ireland much more seriously.

I have continued to question the Justice Minister regarding appropriate sentences for animal abusers. It is important to show that we take animal cruelty seriously and to deter those who would engage in such activity. The fact that those who perpetrated the act of cruelty against Cody were the first to receive custodial sentences for such an offence proves that attitudes are slowly changing.

The Green Party has also been campaigning to have circuses that use wild animals banned in Northern Ireland. I personally believe that not only are circuses a cruel and degrading way for animals to live, but they also send out completely the wrong message to children about how we should treat animals. Our developing understanding of animal welfare now means that we know what they need in order to thrive; physically and psychologically.

Conditions for good welfare include; freedom of movement, ability to perform natural behaviours such as foraging, hunting and dust bathing. Also, the need to have control over situations, such as being able to escape from frightening events like crowds or loud noises and the avoidance, where possible, of generally stressful experiences, such as transportation and cramped living spaces.

With the best will in the world, these conditions cannot be met in the environment of a travelling circus and, therefore, the welfare of animals suffers. Life for circus animals consists of being housed in trucks (restricted to the maximum size of lorry permitted on roads) and small barren temporary enclosures for 90-99% of the day. The enclosures used are, on average, a quarter the size of those recommended for zoos.

Some animals are simply tethered to a peg in the ground, unable to move beyond a few metres, or socialise with others. Loading and transport are stressful even for animals that are experienced; those that on a weekly basis for the 5-10 months circuses travel around the country being loaded and unloaded on a regular basis.

The Green Party in Northern Ireland

made a manifesto commitment to raise standards of animal welfare in Northern Ireland across all sectors from domestic pets, through to indigenous wildlife. We want Northern Ireland to lead the way when it comes to protecting vulnerable animals from unnecessary suffering, and we believe that a ban on wild animals in circuses will be a good step forward. There is overwhelming public support for the banning of wild animals in circuses, as it is the morally and ethically correct thing to do. Animal abuse must be tackled in every circumstance where it occurs.

I am a strong defender of animal welfare because wild animals, farm animals and our domestic pets are sentient beings capable of feeling fear and pain. Animals are vulnerable to so much abuse and cruelty, so we must have proper mechanisms in place to offer them protection. I believe Northern Ireland needs a 24-hour, 365 days dedicated hotline to make reporting animal cruelty much easier. Animal cruelty must be treated like every other crime, so when it is reported, a crime reference number should be issued so progress can be easily monitored.

Other forms of animal cruelty persist in Northern Ireland such as dog fighting, cock fighting and badger baiting. These are often conducted by organised gangs involved in other forms of criminal activity. It's important to recognise that those who perpetrate crimes against animals are more likely to commit crimes against people. Of course, crimes against animals should be taken seriously in their own right.

A register of those convicted of animal cruelty would go some way to ensuring abusers cannot get access to other animals they may mistreat. People convicted of animal abuse should not be permitted to keep more pets as they too are then at risk of abuse and or neglect.

An animal abuser register will allow charities, rehoming centres, the police and other agencies to check more effectively, and quickly if a person has previous convictions for animal cruelty. This register should be available only to responsible organisations that will use it to prevent animals being placed with those who have previously abused or neglected other pets.

There should be ban on fox and stag hunting and an end the use of animals MacMilin circuses as well as a stop put to puppy farming. We also need to have strict controls in the breeding and selling of animals - our wonderful animal sanctuaries are full to capacity with unwanted and abandoned animals; including larger animals such as horses and ponies.

A society can be measured by how it treats animals and more legal protection, dedicated resources and better education are required to ensure in Northern Ireland that we don't fall short of our duty to protect animals. As Leader of the Green Party, and with the support of party members, activists, and citizens, I intend to keep working hard to make sure measures are put in place to protect animals in Northern Ireland.

We have all been touched by the atrocity of what happened to Cody. It was a senseless, and despicable act of violence inflicted on a defenceless family loved pet. I believe that we all need to consider much more broadly as well, how we treat all animals in our society. The reality, as we all know it, is that our society is responsible for grievous inflictions of cruelty towards animals for pleasure in blood sports, through testing of cosmetics on animals and our enslavement of animals in circuses and sea parks. Due to the demands that we place on our planet to fuel our endlessly growing economy, 200 species of plant and animal life go extinct every day.

I'm sure I wouldn't be alone in considering this, not only in the category of cruelty inflicted on the natural world, but as a moral tragedy on an epic scale. Our treatment of animals is reflective of our broader treatment of each other. It's exactly the same lack of empathy that enables those who inflict senseless cruelty towards animals, that also enables people to inflict cruelty towards the elderly or children or people from different races and religions.

This link between cruelty towards animals and the infliction of cruelty on vulnerable people is widely acknowledged. As the philosopher, Immanuel Kant stated:
'We can judge the heart of a man by his treatment of animals. He who is cruel to animals becomes hard also in his dealings with men.'

We must recognise that animals belong to the most vulnerable of all the downtrodden in our society, and animal rights represent the purest form of social justice. Tackling this injustice and understanding the causes of animal cruelty will enable us to better understand and reduce cruelty in our society.
While what happened to poor Cody was disgusting and terrible, I believe we can draw some hope and solace from how people pulled together to make sure that something positive emerged from something so negative. The Agnews are heroes for channelling their grief, sorrow and natural anger, into positive actions that will help all animals in Northern Ireland. Along with the support of the Green Party, we will ultimately carry this message across the whole of the UK and to

the rest of the world.
If we can work together to achieve this, then Cody's suffering will not be in vain, and that those who choose cruelty over kindness will not win.

**Steven Agnew**

Steven Agnew was elected leader of the Green Party in Northern Ireland in January 2011. Originally from Dundonald (just outside Belfast), he was elected Member of the Legislative Assembly for North Down in May 2011, where he has lived for the past five years.

Steven sits on the Enterprise, Trade and Investment Committee, and has been a member of the All Party Group for Children and Young People for the past four years. As a father of two young children, and in full support of Green Party core principals, Steven puts the welfare of children at the top of his agenda.

He is currently bringing forward a Private Member's Bill to the Northern Ireland Assembly, which if passed will create a statutory duty on local government departments to co-operate with children's services.

Steven has also been a long-standing champion of integrated education in Northern Ireland and an ardent supporter of animal welfare issues.

# CHAPTER EIGHT – What's Next?

I still can't believe, to this day, that my family and beloved, innocent pet, Cody, were subjected to such a barbaric, evil and unnecessary act of cruelty of the worst kind. I don't think I will ever come to terms with this; I have tried many times and failed. This is one of the reasons I have to keep going, to keep pushing and fighting for tougher sentencing for animal abusers and continuing to fundraise for animal sanctuaries and charities. This helps me to vent my emotions and keeps me focused on the positive aspects I've drawn from such a horrific event. On reflection, I find it quite surreal when I think back to the day of the attack and the investigation that followed. Then there was the public outrage and all the support, including the instant response of 70,000 supporters on the Facebook page - Justice for Cody. It was such a busy time with all the events that took place during the same period of time. The amount of fundraising that went on was incredible, and then there was the Stormont event, the trial - and finally, the day I longed for and was so determined to get...the final sentencing.

In many ways, I've tried to take many positives from the whole ordeal; it's a coping mechanism I use during any traumatic event. Cody has made me realise what a strong and determined person I am, and this has given me the strength to deal with many other aspects or problems in my life. I see Cody as the voice for all other animals, she has set a brand-new landmark for tougher sentences to be handed out to other animal abusers. She's inspired and driven so many people to stand up and fight.

Cody has brought together 70,000 people on Facebook, many of whom have become friends to us through the site. The support and encouraging words from all the supporters have been my strength and inspiration throughout the last two years. I have no doubt that without every one of the supporters I wouldn't have got as far as I did - for that, I will be eternally grateful. This helped restore my faith in humanity, enabling me to see that not everyone is bad. There's a lot of good out there. There were so many kind gifts sent to us while Cody was at the vets: there were dog coats for her, food, natural healing remedies, lots of cards and well-wishes. These all warmed my heart and made me feel like it wasn't just our family that felt the pain, but a whole nation of animal lovers.

A few people started raising funds for Cody's vet bills, setting up online donation sites. Finally, when Cody didn't make it, all the family decided to use this money to raise further funds for animal sanctuaries. We purchased Cody merchandise and donated the items to various charities, who could sell them and keep the profits for their animals in need. Not only did this raise much-needed revenue for the charities, it also meant Cody's name lived on. She would always be remembered; this was, and still is, very important to me.

The reason we raised a further £5000, to name a guide dog puppy 'Cody', was another way to ensure Cody's legacy didn't die. I wanted to spread awareness to everyone out there that a dog can be completely life-changing to a blind, or partially blind, person. Their quality of life is much better with a guide dog and loving companion, the work these dogs do fascinate me, and their training is remarkable. I thought, if people could be educated about the importance of these dogs, then maybe this could help prevent animal abuse. This would hopefully enable people who have no compassion or experience with animals to see how intelligent and devoted they can be.

*Sunday Life, 28 July 2013*

*"It was a moment of joy for a family who suffered a traumatic tragedy.*

*Thanks to Guide Dogs NI, Spirit of Northern Ireland finalist Natalie Agnew last Monday met the guide dog pup she raised money to fund in memory of her pet dog, Cody, who died after being set alight by heartless yobs close to her Maghaberry home.*

*Almost a year after the horror attack that shocked Northern Ireland, Natalie gave her beloved dog a fitting memorial, by using donations to pay for a new guide dog, named Cody.*

*More than £10,000 poured in from a shocked public after Cody's brutal death, which inspired Natalie to launch a charity fund for animal welfare – eventually totalling over £20,000.*

*Natalie and her husband Martin, and two children, Justin and Jake, along with their new pup, Rex, went along to meet Cody. Said Natalie, "It was emotional and exciting at the same time. It was strange when the trainer kept calling the dog Cody, but at the same time, lovely, because something good has come of it."*

Unfortunately, the impact Cody's attack and death had on my boys is still ongoing. I have found it very difficult and emotional dealing with issues surrounding the boys in relation to this. I do feel their innocent minds were corrupted, and I'm not sure they will ever come to terms with it. I don't think I ever can either. How can anyone come to terms with something so barbaric? I just keep focusing on the campaign for tougher sentences and animal offenders' list, which I would love to be called 'Cody's Law'. I want people to remember Cody for all the good that has come because of her, and so that Cody's name lives on.

I now know in my heart that I did everything possible to bring these culprits to justice, and hopefully preventing them from harming or killing any other animal or human - in the future.

I feel we have justice, to some degree. I strongly think prison sentences should be longer for this type of hideous crime and will continue to fight for that. I know we got the best outcome we possibly could, within the laws of our justice system. Despite this, my family is still left with the unbearable image of our beloved pet Cody and her horrific injuries inflicted unnecessarily. We will carry that for the rest of our lives.

A big thank you to our police investigator who, for security reasons, cannot be named. Without his heartfelt effort and time into this investigation, and his passion for animals, we would not have got this case to trial. Also, a big thank you to all the Cody supporters' friends and families who helped with fundraising and lots more. Again, this would have been impossible without their contribution.

I will continue my fight for tougher sentencing and hope Cody will be remembered worldwide. The last thing I want is for her suffering to be in vain.

*The end was just the beginning ...*